DAN CRARY
The Flatpicker's guide

**Includes Cross-Picking • Playing Accompaniment
Special Techniques-Licks and Runs
Creating Breaks and Instrumental Arrangements to Songs
Plus 23 Full Arrangements**

ISBN 978-1-57424-058-0
SAN 683-8022

cats

Contents

Cover Photo-Doug Kisner
Airbrush-Marshall Vandruff
Calligraphy-George Ports
Paste up-Wes Middlebrook
Layout and Production-Ron Middlebrook

- Introduction -
A personal word from Dan Crary

Before we get started, I'd like to say a word directly from me to you. This is not just another guitar instruction book. If I thought it was, I wouldn't have bothered with it. My goal in writing this particular book is to help you make music, GOOD music, the beautiful, soul-satisfying, fun, interesting, personal music that flatpicking can be. This is intended to be a book that WORKS. If it failed to work for you, I would not be satisfied. So I have poured everything into the thinking and writing of this book that I could.

In addition, this is a very personal approach to flatpicking. Included are the best ideas for solving problems and making progress that I know. Most of my own information, the tricks, the ideas, the ways of playing that work for me are here. This is the straight shoot, the inside stuff, banged out by me at home on a rather old typewriter with two fingers (sorry, I never got out of the "open position" on the typewriter).

Because the contents are MY approach, they are not just theoretical, they are concrete and they work, most of the time. That doesn't mean that some other approach to a particular part of your playing wouldn't work just as well. But at least the materials here have come from my own struggles with the challenges of flatpicking since 1952, and they have been tested and refined in the laboratory of private instruction (which I used to have time for) and the hundreds of workshops I have conducted all over the USA and foreign countries.

My editor, and the president of Centerstream Publications, Ron Middlebrook and I have done our best to put flatpicking information in an accurate, interesting, and learnable form in these pages. We welcome any comments and questions you might write to us, and we sincerely wish you good hunting as you get into the good stuff we have packed into the following pages.

Sincerely,

Dan Crary

CD Track list:
1. Introduction/John Henry
2. Rovin' Gambler
3. 9 Pound Hammer
4. Little Sadie
5. Soldiers Joy, Part 1
6. Soldiers Joy, Part 2
7. Bill Cheatum, Part 1
8. Bill Cheatum, Part 2
9. Fisher's Hornpipe, Part 1, Basic Version
10. Fisher's Hornpipe, Part 2,
11. Fisher's Hornpipe, Part 1, Advanced Version
12. Fisher's Hornpipe, Part 2,
13. Part 4, Banjo Pattern 1 & 2
14. "In The Mood" Pattern
15. "Back and Forth" Pattern
16. Banjo Pattern/Beaumont Rag
17. Home, Sweet Home, Part 1 & 2
18. Wabash Cannonball
19. Section 4b - "G" runs #1, 2 & 3
20. The "Treble" Run
21. The Golden Era Run
22. "Banjo" Runs #1, 2, 3, 4
23. The "Shot Jackson" Run
24. The "Peaches & Herb" Run
25. The "Piano Blues" Run
26. The "Slash" Licks
27. The "Floating" Run & "Cascade" Run
28. The "Chain" Run, The "Double Stop" Run, The "Clarence White" Run
29. 4C Gold Rush
30. Section 5, "Repertoire Building", Flop-Eared Mule
31. Ragtime Annie
32. Red Haired Boy
33. Reuben
34. Done Gone
35. Dill Pickle Rag
36. Blackberry Blossom
37. Lady's Fancy
38. The Dusty Miller
39. Lime Rock
40. Huckleberry Hornpipe

FLATPICKING
A short history

"Flatpicking" is much more than just playing the guitar with a single pick or "plectrum" as the pick is termed in formal music terms. Flatpicking is a whole approach to the guitar which uses the plectrum, but uses it to accomplish something that marks the music which results as unique and special. The combination of the large-body, steel-string guitar, the pick, and the approach or style of flatpicking has produced a kind of music which stands on its own as one of the most recognizeable and powerful guitar styles heard today.

Maybe the best way to define Flatpicking is to say a word about where it came from and who the main flatpickers are. The musical context of most flatpicking has been American traditional music, especially Bluegrass, with roots in the old-time country music band of the past sixty years or so. The guitar was usually a rhythm instrument in the old time bands, but a few guitarists from those days pioneered a more "up front" role for the instrument with some early experiments in playing runs and leads. Some of those early heroes who saw their guitars as more than just rhythm instruments included Riley Puckett, Roy Harvey, Leonard Copeland, Jess Harvey, Maybelle Carter, Bill and Earl Bolick, Charlie Monroe, and Jimmie Rodgers.

But the real birth of flatpicking was in Bluegrass music. At the end of World War II Bill Monroe had made some personnel changes in his "Bluegrass Boys" band at the Grand Ole Opry to include Lester Flatt on guitar, Earl Scruggs on banjo, Chubby Wise on fiddle, and as always, himself on mandolin. These musicians working together created the combination of instrumental styles and singing that resulted in what we recognize today as Bluegrass music. Even in the early "Bluegrass Boys" the guitar took a supporting role, playing only rhythm. But as the music caught on and other bands formed to play the music, the guitar was occasionally heard playing a lead.

In the 1950's Earl Scruggs (later in partnership with Lester Flatt and the Foggy Mountain Boys) sometimes laid aside his banjo to finger-pick a break on the guitar during a gospel song. By the late 1950's, a few guitar soloists were making regular appearances in Bluegrass music and they were using the plectrum in styles that represent the first real "flatpicking".

The Stanley Brothers had featured Charlie Cline on a few guitar solos, and by 1958 they made the lead guitar a permanent part of their show, first with Bill Napier and later with George Shuffler, whose solo playing was heard in virtually everything that band recorded. But it was for a banjo player to claim the distinction of recording the first flatpicking instrumental record: Don Reno of Reno and Smiley (who once told me his first love was the lead guitar) recorded "Contry Boy Rock 'N Roll" in 1959 and played the most sophisticated Bluegrass flatpicking ever heard at the time.

By the decade of the sixties, however, flatpicking almost had to be re-invented, Reno had gone back to the banjo and Bluegrass was still a music known to a relatively small segment of Americans. To do the job it took two giants whose names today are almost synonyms for flatpicking: Clarence White (of the Kentucky Colonels, later of the Byrds) and Doc Watson. By the mid-sixties Clarence White had recorded a series of tunes featuring the flatpicked guitar in a bluegrass band that was agreed to be a supreme statement of guitar power and finesse. And Doc Watson emerged from the folk music revival of the time to become one of the greatest traditional singer-guitarists of any age who became known internationally as the great master and popularizer of Flatpicking.

My own opportunity to become a part of flatpicking came in 1968, when our band, the Bluegrass Alliance started making festival appearances and recording the first flatpicking album which announced that it was **guitar** music, with other instruments in support. Stepping from the ranks of session players, Norman Blake began touring and recording as a soloist with a mighty flatpick, And in 1970, the world got its first look at flatpicker Tony Rice who would come to establish himself as one of the great players in the history of the guitar.

Looking back on our first thirty years or so, it's important to recognize flatpicking as something rather new. This means that you have an opportunity to be in on the developmental days of a guitar style that shows signs of long and continued growth and influence. As part of that, you have an opportunity to actually see and hear many of the artists who helped to create this music in person, as well to hear much of our history on relatively modern recordings.

As you work through this book and practice your guitar, one of the best things you could do for your playing is to **listen** to flatpicking, Check over the discograghy below, get as wide a variety of classic flatpicking records as you can, and listen, listen, listen until the music is a part of you. Whenever a good flatpicker is appearing within a couple hundred miles or so, buy a ticket and watch and listen. The experience will inspire you and advance your own playing far beyond what this book alone can do. And as you think of our short history, don't forget to include yourself as part of it. Flatpickers stick together, they're loyal to each other, and they help each other learn. I have played and jammed with fellow flatpickers from more than twenty countries, and they are the same everywhere: they all feel like what they're doing is special and important. They like to get together with other guitar players and know that they're part of an international group of colleagues and friends who are together in making flatpicking a beautiful and powerful new music. I'm proud to welcome you to that group. And you have some great guitar music and good times ahead of you.

Getting the most from this book

Level and approach

This book is designed especially for intermediate players who want to improve technique, solve the common problems of learning the guitar, and build repertoire with some arrangements of tunes and songs plus ideas for creating one's own breaks, arrangements, licks and runs. If you're a beginner, the book can be used selectively by your teacher as a supplement to other learning materials; if you're working on your own, this book is ideal as a follow-up to a beginning flatpicking book. I have tried to present materials in such a way that you can connect with the book wherever you are now, and in such a way that it will advance your playing to levels which are interesting, satisfying, and challenging. Throughout, I have tried to give you the real, inside story, the real issues and the best solutions and approaches I know. I don't just want to sell you a book. . .I want to improve your playing.

Reading the music notation

Throughout this book you'll find standard music notation accompanied by tablature or TAB. I've done that so you can follow the text, whatever your preference in notation. If you're a note reader be sure to check the tab as the tab supplements the standard notation with information about technique, which frets and strings to choose, picking direction, and suggestions for fingerings. Here are the main aspects of TAB illustrated:

1. Frets and Strings: The horizontal lines represent the six strings of the guitar, the top line is the first string. Numbers on these lines indicate a fret number to be fingered with the left hand.

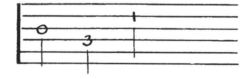

In the above example, the TAB tells you to play three notes: third string open, fourth string fretted at the third fret, and second string fretted at the first fret.

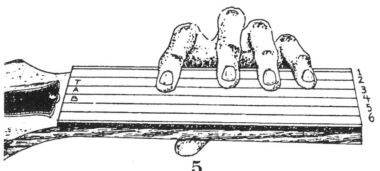

2. Timing. Unless otherwise indicated, each note of the TAB is a "quarter note" receiving one beat in a four-beat measure.
The measure:. . .would be counted

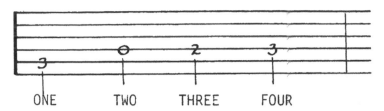

ONE   TWO   THREE   FOUR

If the notes are indicated as follows, they are "eighth notes", played two-per-beat, or twice as fast.
This measure:. . .would be counted:

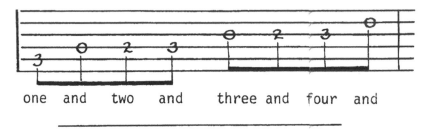

one and two and   three and four and

---

3. Picking Direction: As a general rule, it's a very good idea to pick **down** ↓ on the main beats and **up** ↑ whenever a note occurs on the "and" after a beat.

For example:. .

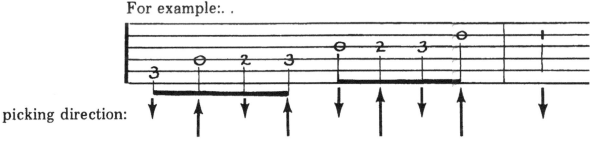

picking direction:

The reason for this rule is that a consistent picking direction helps you keep timing straight, and frees you from having to **decide which direction to pick each note every time you play.**

---

4. Fingering: Occasionally, the TAB will indicate left-hand fingering. As in this example.

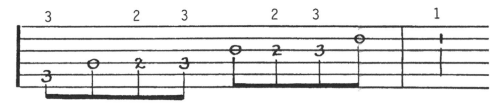

The numbers over each note in the TAB indicated which finger of the left hand to use. When fingering is not indicated, especially when playing in the open position, ordinarily use the finger whose number corresponds to the fret number (third finger on the third fret, etc.)

---

5. "Hammering-On", "Pulling-Off", "Sliding" and "Bends"

Hammering-on means to sound a note not by picking it, but by fingering the indicated position **hard.** The string hits the fret hard enough to make it vibrate and sound the note.

Pulling-off means that one note is fretted, then the next note is played, not by picking it, but by pulling the left-hand finger from the first note's fret in such a way that it "picks" the string, sounding the second note of the two. The pull-off may take you from a fretted note to an open note, or from one fretted note to another.

Sliding means playing a fretted note, then moving the left-hand finger to the next note without taking it off the string, so the notes connect with a rising or falling pitch.

Bending the note means keeping your finger on the note and bending the string up a step (one fret) or a whole step (two frets).

A short passage that might use three of the techniques would look like this:

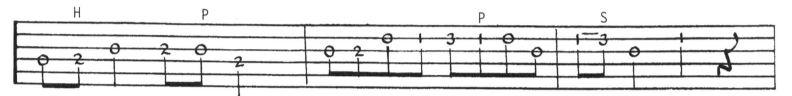

Note: In the above example, notes marked H, P, or S are not picked; they are sounded by the corresponding hammer-on, pull-off, or slide.

---

6. "Rest": A rest indicates a pause in which you play nothing for a specified length of musical time. Rests are used to end or otherwise punctuate a phrase, or sometimes for "syncopation". a "quarter rest" ⌡ gets one beat whenever the music notation assigns one beat to a "quarter note". In other words, a "quarter rest" gets the same time as a quarter note; an eighth rest ⅞ indicates a pause the same length as an eighth note.

---

7. Natural Harmonic:
The fret hand lightly touches the string over a designated fret. Then it is struck. A chime-like sound is produced.

Use of Appendices

The appendices are provided for reference and study when needed. In your first read-through of this book, please read the appendices so you'll have an idea of what's there when you need it.

Appendix A relates directly to Chapter 3.

Appendix C relates to Chapter 1.

Appendix B is for those of us needing special help with right-hand technique.

Appendix D has some ideas to help you in choosing and caring for a guitar.

Getting the most out of practice

Over the years I've known a lot of flatpickers. I think I can say that I know what we're all like pretty well. One of the things I've learned about us is that what we call "practice" often isn't. In fact there are a lot of misconceptions about what practice is and what it can do. I'd like to get us all to think about practice a little differently, and help our playing in the bargain.

Here are a few points to consider:

1. Practice is **not** playing for fun. I don't mean to be an old grouch about this, but what most of us call "practice" is just sort of fooling around for fun. If somebody says "I practiced for three hours today" he or she may mean, "I sat back comfortably and doodled around all afternoon." Well, friends, here's the old grouch in me. . .playing like that, aimlessly, randomly, purposelessly is one of the worst things you can do for your playing, especially if it becomes a substitute for practice. On the other hand, there is fun and satisfaction to be accomplished in serious, productive practice. So please read on...

2. Another misconception about practice: if it's long and repetitious it works more effectively. Someone in a workshop said one time, "I guess it's just practice, practice, practice". Well, not exactly. It's possible to hammer away at something so long that you just make things worse, go past the point of diminishing returns, drive yourself crazy with it. It's important not to over-do it, to know when you've reached your limit. But enough on what practice isn't; how about what it **is**...

3. Each practice session, **set a goal.** Decide what you would like to accomplish **today.** It may be something small, such as cleaning up one short rough spot in a tune or learning half of one verse of a new break, or polishing up one run. But make it a **reachable** goal, one that you can stay with long enough to experience the satisfaction of knowing you moved forward, today. Even a short few minutes spent reaching a small but significant goal is better practice than hours spent without direction or trying to reach some distant or unrealistic objective. To put it another way, figure out where you want to go then proceed incrementally, in steps, one step today, another tomorrow, and so on.

4. Practice like you would study anthing new. Be comfortable, but not too comfortable. That old roll-up-your-sleeves attitude that is a combination of determination, alertness, and concentration will serve you well. If possible, prepare a quiet place where the main activity is serious study, go there armed with study materials from an instructor or something like this book, have a goal in mind, pour yourself a cup of coffee, and get down to business.

5. Last, let me say to you that learning the guitar is an adventure not to be taken lightly. The guitar itself is deceptive: it's easy to play just a little, but difficult to play well. That means that a combination of hard work and patience is very important. And it means that the satisfaction of getting somewhere is **very** satisfying. If you love the instrument you know what I mean; it doesn't matter whether you're a pro or semi-pro or a serious amateur or a closet player, guitar music is elusive, subtle, not easily achieved, and wonderfully rewarding. I'm convinced that playing well is not so much a technique as it is a decision. It's a commitment to do the work, strive for concentration, get strategic about advancing by steps, and push patiently forward toward the goal.

Sometimes the rewards come in small coins, but they shine with the unmistakable quality of 24 karats.

Playing Accompaniment

Backup playing is a neglected subject in flatpicking literature. Part of the problem is that flatpickers are very hung up on lead playing, the spotlight, the glory, the roar of the crowd, and all that. As a result, we sometimes don't think much about variations in our accompaniment styles. Another part of the problem is that audiences listen to what's out front, but often don't notice unusual or tasty back-ground licks. Maybe if the former were less true, the latter would be less of a problem. Anyway, to clean up and spice up your rhythm playing, here are some of my ideas.

Ex.1

But first, I'd like to introduce you to the most **original** accompaniment lick in flatpicking, one that is almost never heard, one which may be the most effective of all:

Wait a minute, you're saying; is something missing? Yes, this is the simplest of all 4/4 time accompaniment licks, the "boom-chick" or bass-strum lick. What's missing is all the extra, messy stuff we often throw in unsystematically and randomly, with disasterous results. My point is this: as we examine some variations below, let's keep this pattern in mind as something we should go back to **often** (every couple of measures or so). This pattern should be like home base with the excursions below seen as short forays which are not allowed to become so long they become monotonous. The best guitar players know that their job in a band is to make the rhythm solid and clean primarily.

There is a rule for this pattern: The first note of the measure should be the same note (the tonic) of the chord. Notice that each note and strum is given the rhythmic value of a quarter note, and is played with a downstroke.

Ex.2

Now, check the first variation on this pattern- **playing an eighth-note after the strum:**

Be sure to notice that I have **not** written this rhythmic variation with two eighth-note strums, which is the way it's often taught to people.

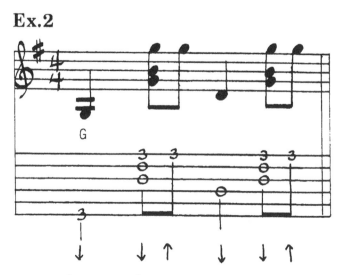

Ex.3

The upstroke after the strum should not be another strum, because that makes it too clumsy to control, and it adds too much clutter to the measure. In Ex. 2, notice how the upstroke on just the first string following the strum gives a much cleaner-and equally full-sound. It's also easier to play.

Here's an idea you may not have thought of: Instead of putting in an eighth-note after the strum, try putting one in after the **bass** note. It can be on the same string, as in Ex.4. or even better, play the extra note on a different string, as shown in Ex.5. When used once in a while, this little variation sounds very different, provides a lot of variety, and is easy to execute with a little practice. It works well even in very fast tempos.

Ex.4

Ex.5

The next variation I suggest is a combination of Ex.2. and Ex.5. It involves an upstroke after the bass note **and** the strum, like this:

Ex.6

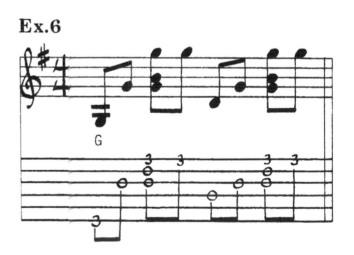

Let me offer a few pointers on using all of these variations. First, notice that the basic bass-strum pattern is still there, unchanged on the counts of one, two, three, and four. The extra notes have been sneaked in between the main beats on the "and" counts. Practice these slowly enough so that the basic pattern still comes through. Secondly, use them as variations-move in and out of them to provide variety as you're playing a phrase or a tune.

Now here are some other less systematic, but equally effective techniques to drop into your playing. The first involves substituting a strum in place of the bass note:

Ex.7

Or, instead of a downward strum, try an upward strum on the first beat. It's the same idea shown in Ex.7, but it utilizes a quick downward arpeggio the first string to the sixth string, with the pick snapping up off of the sixth string to emphasize the low G note as the first beat of the next measure. This would look something like this:

Ex.8

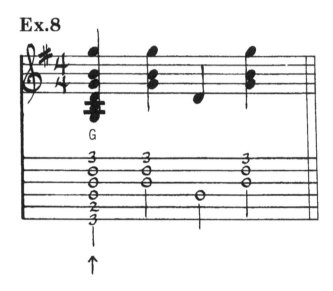

For a slightly off-beat accompaniment lick, try using eighth-note rest on the first and third beats:

Ex.9

One other suggestion: When using an alternating bass-note and strum pattern, don't strum the whole chord. Try strumming only the top three strings and see how much cleaner it comes out; the patterns should sound neat, and not cluttered. Sometimes the best variety is achieved by using no variations, playing the basic lick straight and unembellished.

Consider the following syncopated combination of "splashes" or strums which is a sort of **accompaniment power-play.**

This is a hard-driving, punchy sort of backup lick which can help to drive home a powerful and/or fast spot in your music. It's two measures long: you might want to count it as eight beats, as shown:

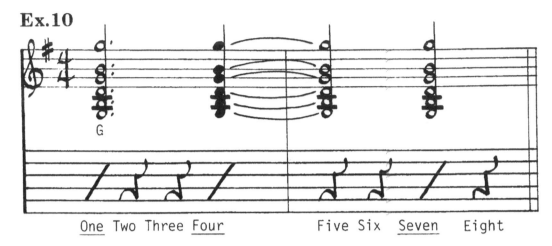

One Two Three Four   Five Six Seven Eight

Actually, there's a bit more to it than that. You may want to practice the Ex.10 version with the rests just to get it straight, but then in place of the rests you can put in some light strums or "tickles" of the chord for fullness. Something like this:

One final word about these variations in the basic rhythm lick: **any change you introduce in the back-up of a piece of music will get the audience's attention.** This could be a problem if attention is called to the rhythm and away from the soloist whose break or lead is supposed to be the focus of attention. So work toward this goal: **work toward the use of variations in accompaniment which call attention not to themselves, but to what the soloist is doing.** For example, in a standard "verse and chorus" fiddle tune, you might soften up a little toward the end of the verse and then play harder when the soloist gets to the chorus, for the purpose of calling attention to the shift in the tune. Or maybe there's a place in your banjo player's break on a familiar piece where he or she softens up a bit and you can do the same. Again the point is, changes in accompaniment can call attention to themselves, or to the lead music being played. Your fellow band members will love you for keeping it solid and simple part of the time, and using the variations to highlight what the soloist is trying to accomplish.

Creating Breaks To Songs

It's difficult to imagine, but only a few years ago it was unusual to hear a break or lead played in bluegrass or traditional music. It had been done, of course (see our section "Flatpicking" p.4), but it was the exception to the rule that breaks were played on fiddle or banjo. Even in Bluegrass, where flatpicking has found its most widespread acceptance, guitar breaks in songs have become some sort of norm only since about 1970.

This section of this book, I must confess, was a tough one for me to write, because creating a break for a song is a highly individual sort of thing, not easily systematized. This section will take the approach of getting you started in a direction that will ultimately help you create your own approach to creating breaks to songs.

One of the milestones in my early playing was something whch came along on the radio in Kansas City in about 1953. There was a fellow named Bud Hunt on the "Brush Creek Follies", a live country music show on the old KMBC Radio. They introduced Bud that night to play a tune I'd never heard, "Wildwood Flower". Fortunately, I had my old wire (!) recorder running, because from that tune I learned how to hammer-on, and how to begin playing guitar breaks.

Let me show you how it worked for me.
The melody of "Wildwood Flower" goes something like this:

Notice that there are several places where the melody pauses or holds a sustained note for extra beats. The approach of Maybelle Carter, Jimmie Rodgers, and others was to add chord strums where the melody pauses or holds, creating what is surely the classic approach to playing a break on a traditional song. Here is how "Wildwood Flower" sounds with the chords added:

Although Flatpicking has moved in a more "Linear" or melodic direction that this "Carter Family" approach, this is still a good place to begin creating breaks for songs; it still sounds good, bands like Flatt and Scruggs have used it very effectively, and it can be the basis from which to move on to more complex breaks.

Let's try a standard song like "John Henry". The melody of John Henry played in a straight melody-plus-chords, or Carter Family style would look like this:

John Henry

Key of G

Traditional, arranged by Dan Crary

14

15

As you look at the following arrangement of the same tune, look for the differences in the two versions. Notice that in place of quarter notes, some eighth notes have been subsitituted. But not just random eighth notes, they should have a couple of qualities: a). the subsitituted quarter notes should SUGGEST or work around the melody, and b). the eighth notes group themselves into clusters or passages that can be thought of as runs or licks. See if you can pick some of these out as you work on this arrangement:

John Henry

Key of G

Traditional, arranged by Dan Crary

Now let me point out some of the runs that are imbedded in this arrangement of "John Henry" (all of these runs are discussed in the section of this book beginning on P.44). The tune begins with one version of the "G" run; another version is in measure 4 (note that measures are numbered from the first **complete**, four-beat measure; it's the measure over which the first chord symbol appears). In measures 7 and 8 there is one of the "Banjo" runs we discuss on p. 45 and 46. Measures 16-19 are a version of the "Clarence White" run on p.49 & 50.

So let's sum up what we've done so far...First, we figured out how the basic melody goes, with a few chords inserted where there is a pause. Next, we looked for alternative things to do in place of the quarter notes and chords: we inserted some identifiable standard runs.

Just to nail down the point, let's go through it one more time, this time with the song. "The Rovin' Gambler". First, the basic melody plus chords

Rovin' Gambler

Key of G

Traditional, arranged by Dan Crary

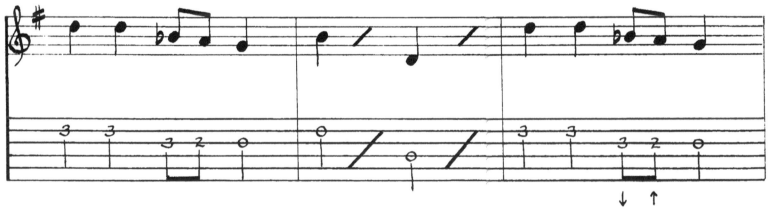

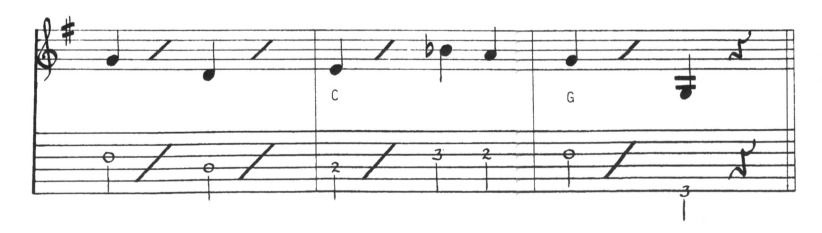

Now taking this basic idea, we add some runs and eighth-note passages to flesh out a full arrangement.

Rovin' Gambler

Key of G

Traditional, arranged by Dan Crary

19

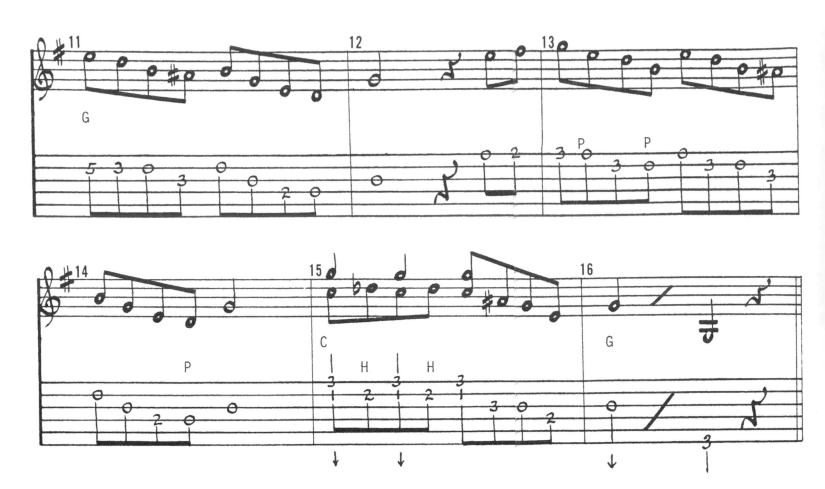

Among the runs we discuss later in the "runs" section which you'll find in this arrangement of "Rovin' Gambler" are: measures 4-8, "Clarence White II"; measure 9, a version of the "G" run; measure 11, part of one of the "banjo" runs; measures 13-14, the "treble" run; and in measure 15, the "slash lick".

Even though you might not want always to depend so heavily on standard runs or licks for your arranging of breaks for songs, they are one place to begin finding ideas. As you become more and more familiar with these breaks, you may experiment around further and modify the arrangements into something less dependent on runs. The point is, begin with what you **can** do, then evolve a break which gets better as you think of additional things to do. The following arrangements are included with their "Carter-Family" versions just to get you started thinking about them; the full arrangements are less dependent on runs, and more on things to do that I thought up over a period of time.

The following arrangements are included with their "Carter-Family" versions just to get you started thinking about them; the full arrangements are less dependent on runs, and more on things to do that I thought up over a period of time.

9 Pound Hammer

Key of G

Traditional, arranged by Dan Crary

9 Pound Hammer

Key of G

Traditional, arranged by Dan Crary

Little Sadie

Key of Dm

Traditional, arranged by Dan Crary

Little Sadie

Key of D minor
Position: OPEN
("Drop D") tuning, DADGBE

Traditional, arranged by Dan Crary

Creating Instrumental Arrangements Of Traditional Tunes

Because most old time traditional music in the frontier United States was played on fiddle and banjo (guitar came along rather late to the American countryside), people still call these old tunes "fiddle tunes" or "banjo tunes". Actually, they're just tunes, and they belong to anyone who can master them on whatever instrument they choose. The point of origin is important, however, because the best versions of these tunes tend to come from the best musicians who are also close to the source, namely, the best fiddlers and banjo players. Thus, I begin this section with a bow to our colleagues who play those instruments and know the great tunes, and with a disclaimer: the following tunes are arranged by a **guitar** player. Therefore, they should be seen as a stepping stone toward your goal of ventually learning these tunes from a fiddle or banjo player directly. In appendix A I give you some ideas about how to do that. In this section I provide you my best efforts at doing what I recommend in the appendix.

Now let's consider some things to do and think about when arranging and playing a traditional tune. First, the arrangement should contain the tune in some sort of complete and original form. But second, it should sound like **GUITAR** music. Given what I said above, that presents the problem of how far to go in either direction. Should it be **very** close to the fiddle or banjo, or further from them in the direction of the guitar? The answer is, it seems to me, that a compromise is ideal. I recommend in appendix A that you work out some tunes directly from fiddle or banjo players. But don't stop there. Let the fiddle or banjo version educate your senses to the tune, then work out a guitar arrangement that fits your instrument. The mistake sometimes made by guitar players is that we rush into a guitar version without having been educated by the original version, or we listen to the fiddle notes and copy them, and leave it there. Neither is very satisfying. The arrangements which follow here (and in section 6) are my attempt to follow my own advice; in each case I learned at least some of the original version note-for-note (usually from a record or personal tape) and then moved into a guitar interpretation which preserved much of the original, but works on the guitar.

Take "Soldier's Joy", for example. In this arrangement there are really two versions written into one, so that you can see how a simple line can be embellished without losing the sense of the tune. As is typical of these tunes, there are two parts; each part consists of eight measures, repeated, for a total of sixteen. Here I have written out all sixteen measures of each part with a simple run of the tune in the first eight and a more complex or embellished or ornamented run of the same melody in the second eight. Thus, you could play the following arrangement three ways:

1. Play it as is.
2. Play only the first eight measures of each part **twice** (this would give you a complete simple version).
3. Play the second set of eight measures in each part twice, giving you a more complex version throughout.

Food for thought: compare the first and second sets of eight measures and think about the differences and similarities you observe. Which do you like better? Do you like both? What techniques are used to make the version more complex or "fancier"? How could these same techniques be used to vary another tune that you know? As you come up with answers to these questions, you'll be developing your own ideas about how to arrange a tune, how to create variations, how to make a tune your own.

Soldier's Joy

Note that in Part 2 the series of notes in measures 9, 10, 13, and 14 are sixteenth-notes, which means that they all happen in the space of one beat. It's difficult to count notes that fast, so the best advice is: **Play them just as fast as you can,** and when you've got them going about as fast as humanly possible, they should just about fall into one beat. The combination of one hammer-on followed by two pull-offs should be worked into a single sort of rolling motion.

Key of D
Position: OPEN

Traditional, arranged by Dan Crary

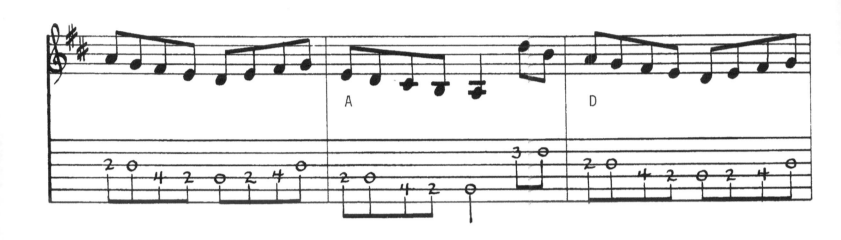

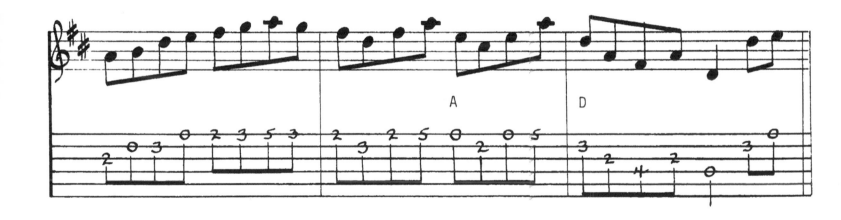

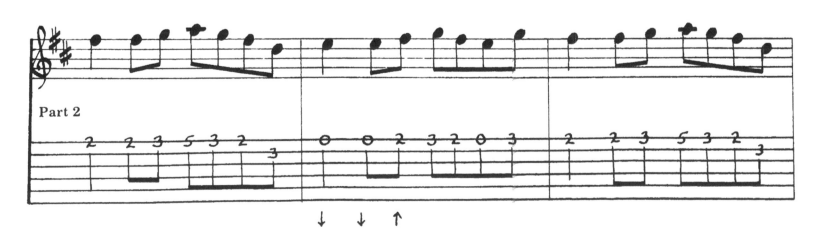

Part 2

28

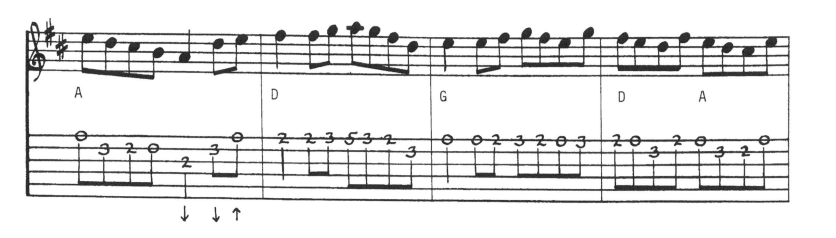

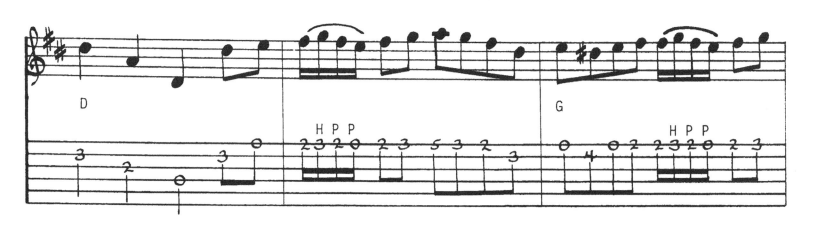

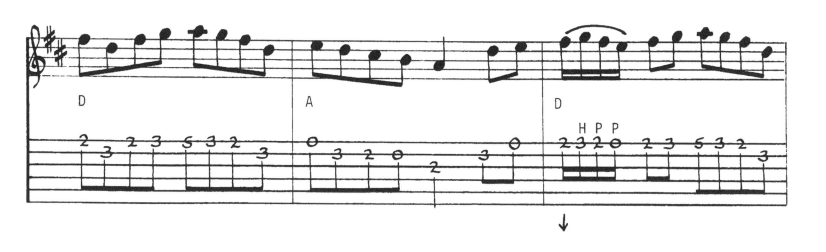

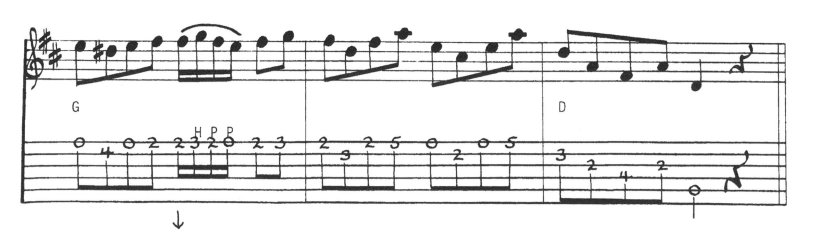

Now let's do the same thing with another well-known tune, "Bill Cheatham". The format is the same: the first eight measures of part 1 are straighter and simpler, the second eight are more complex. The same is true of part 2. Just as in "Soldier's Joy" you can subsititute one set of eight measures for another. But here's another idea; as you decide which passages you like best in this arrangement, try substituting shorter sections for each other. In the early measures of part 1 you can add "8" to the measure number and substitute that later measure at this early spot. For example, when you come to measures 2 and 3, instead of playing them, try measures 10 (2-8) and 11 (3-8). In other words, since there are two versions of the same melody line, any part of one version can be inserted into the other version, so long as it's at the same place in the melody. The point is, learn the whole arrangement, then creatively "fool around" with the ideas, substitute equivalent passages, choose the ones you like, and come up with your own preferred arrangement which you created out of ingredients I've provided here.

Bill Cheatham

Key of A
Capo, 2nd fret

Traditional, arranged by Dan Crary

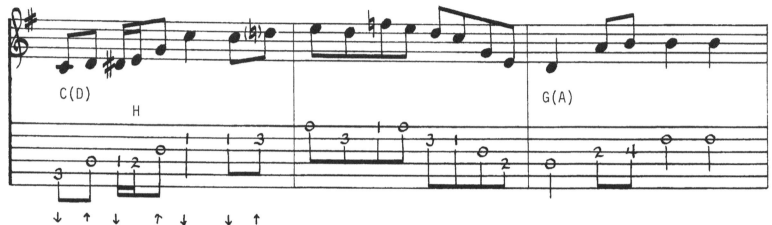

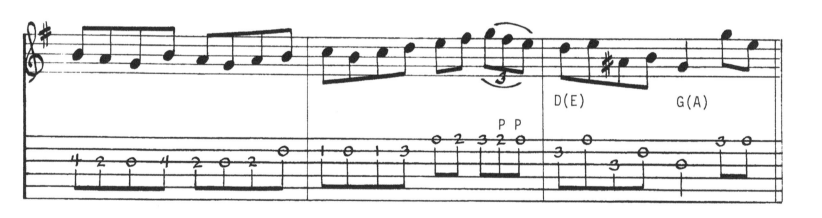

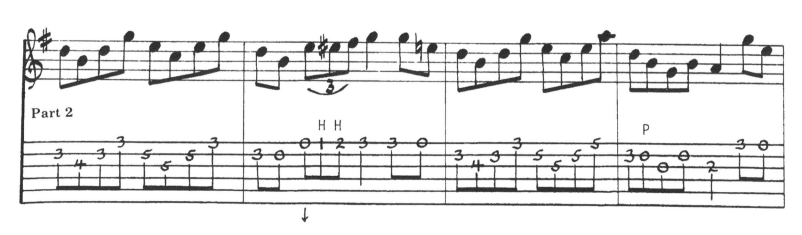

31

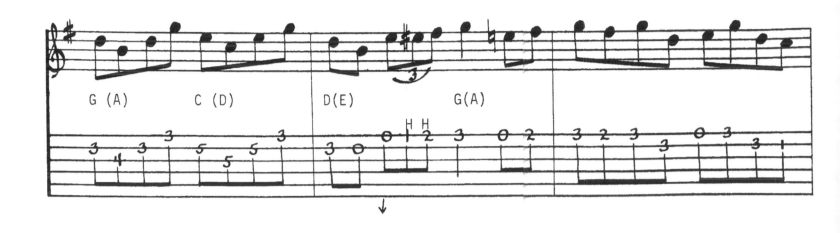

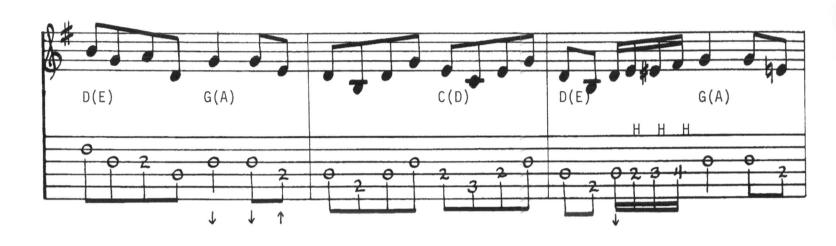

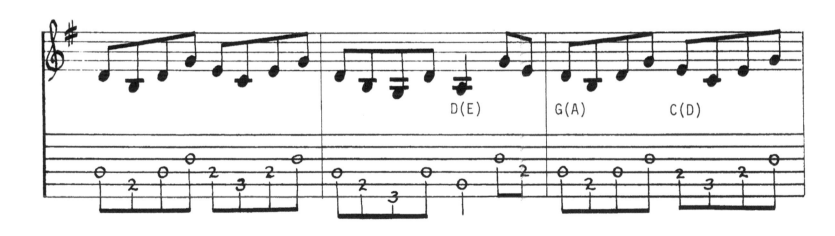

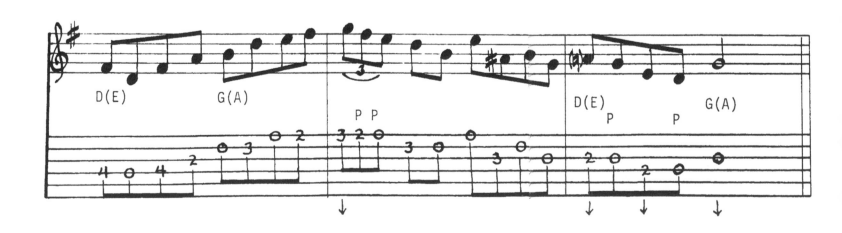

Finally, here are two versions of "Fisher's Hornpipe" for comparison. This time, I have written two **separate** versions. But you can still substitute measures for each other and compare the difference in the measures to gain some ideas about those food-for-thought issues we raised when we discussed "Soldier's Joy".

Fisher's Hornpipe
(Basic Version)

Key of D
Position: OPEN
Tuning: Drop D

Traditional, arranged by Dan Crary

Fisher's Hornpipe
(Advanced Version)

Key of D
Position: OPEN
("Drop D") tuning, DADGBE

Traditional, arranged by Dan Crary

Part 1

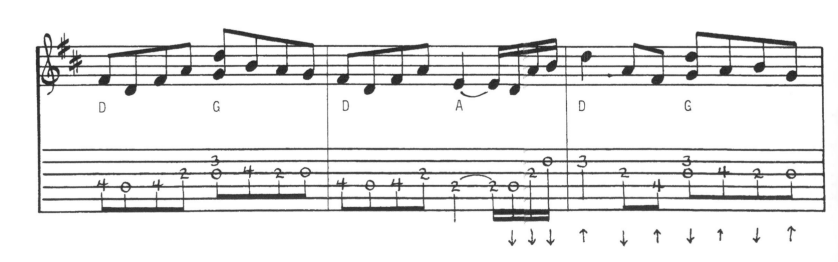

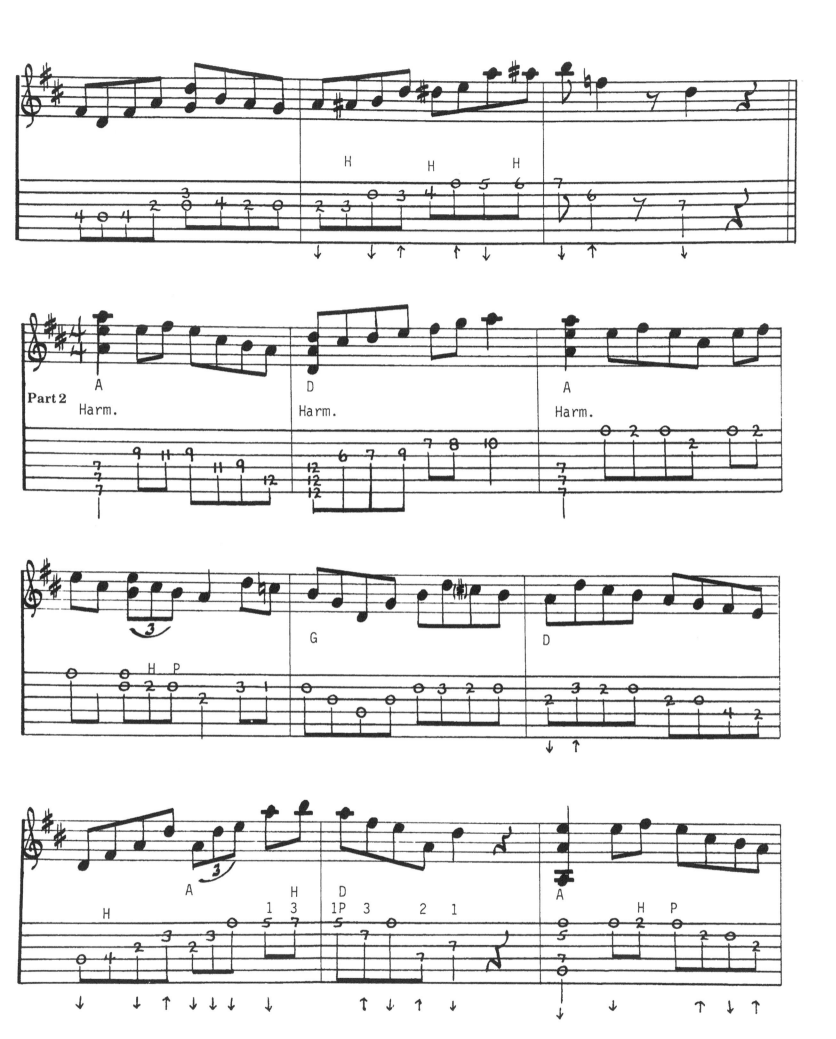

Cross-Picking

One of the most versatile flatpicking techniques is called "cross-picking" in which the pick strikes adjacent strings in a sort of vertical arrangement of notes. The execution and the effect is very similar to what banjo players call a "roll", and some cross-picking patterns are very close to particular banjo rolls.

There is a sort of mystique about this technique which is difficult to explain; it seens that cross-picking has the reputation among guitar players as being very difficult to play, perhaps even more so to understand and apply. But if you look below at a couple of the most commonly used patterns I think you may be pleasantly surprised to find them not so difficult. The trick is to get one or two of the patterns working slowly and steadily until they become **automatic.** Then when the right hand can do the cross-picking pattern by itself, you can turn your attention to making changes in the fingering to make it all come out music. Then we'll try out a tune which includes some cross-picking: "Home Sweet Home".

First, here are a couple of "Banjo" patterns; the first resembles the roll Earl Scruggs plays in the opening measures of "Foggy Mtn. Breakdown" and the second is close to another well-worn banjo roll.

Banjo Pattern 1

Banjo Pattern 2

Note that the picking direction follows the rule of **down on the counts of 1, 2, 3, and 4 and up** on "and". The reason for this is that keeping the picking direction consistent makes it possible to learn one way of doing it every time, and because the even number of picking directions (up and down) played against all those clusters of three notes makes the emphasis shift around to create a nice syncopation. A similar sort of syncopation occurs in the pattern I call the "In The Mood" pattern:

"In The Mood" Pattern

Words and Music by
Joe Garland

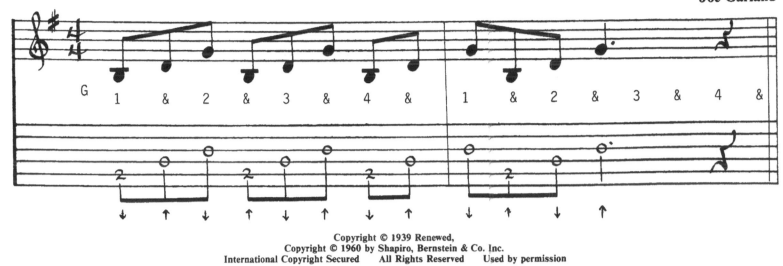

And here's a non-syncopated pattern we'll call the "Back and Forth":

"Back and Forth" Pattern

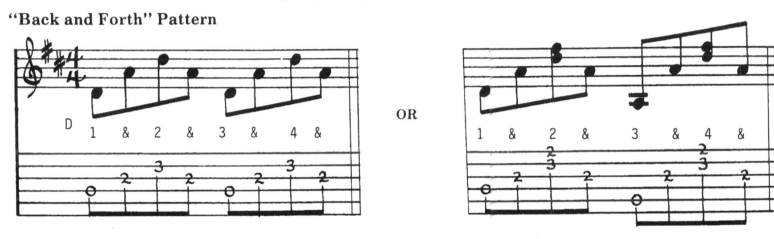

OR

When these patterns begin to feel comfortable and automatic, then here's something to try on your own: Since the patterns will work on any three strings which are fingered in such a way as to make a chord of any kind, experiment around by changing the chords to any three-string combination that sounds good. Then try cross-picking a chord in which you change just the top or bottom note higher or lower,   alternating back and forth each time the particular string is played in the pattern. For example, if you play the "Banjo 2" pattern and vary it by moving the note played on the top string like this example below:

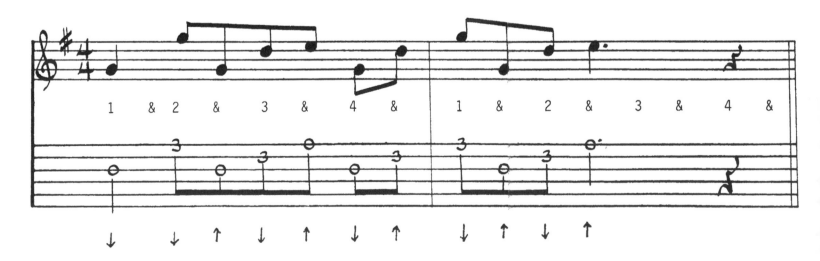

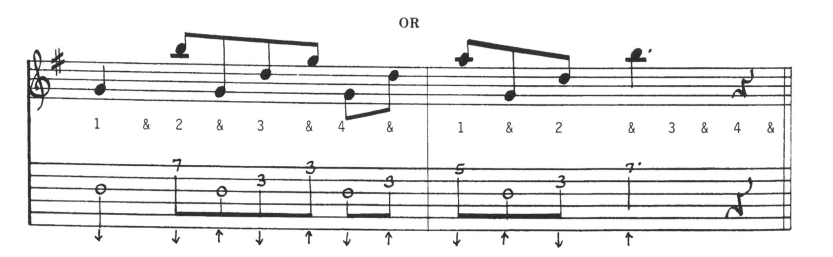

Another example shows how "In The Mood" becomes a line from "Beaumont Rag" by changing just one note with the left hand, while the right continues to play the pattern:

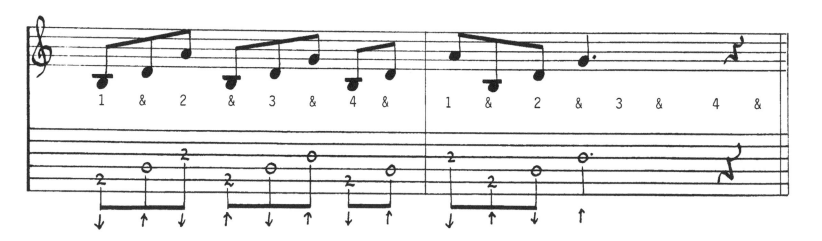

To sum up, these patterns are useful for practice, to get your right hand familiar with some things to do automatically, and they are also useful as something the right hand can do while the left hand is moving around a bit much like a banjo player does. Cross-picking can take the place of a chord strum or rest measure when there is a pause in a melody line, or it can substitute for places when the fiddle plays a "shuffle" in a fiddle tune like "Cotton Patch Rag" or "Beaumont Rag". Cross-picking is an **idea** technique; once you can do it a little you can discover new ways and places to use it by doing your own experimenting.

Now let's look at and play a couple of tunes that use quite a bit of cross-picking. If you look at them closely you will recognize several places where one of the above patterns appears right in the middle of the tune. These tunes should be started slowly, of course, but never need to be played very fast. The relatively slow tempo and the sustained feeling of the cross-picking rolls make these tunes very easy-going and pretty.

Home, Sweet Home

Key of C
Position: OPEN

Traditional, arranged by Dan Crary

Part 1

Like the weather, crosspicking is one of those phenomena that everybody discusses but does nothing about. It's an impressive technique in the sense that it sounds difficult, and indeed it can be tricky to execute. But I rarely hear players using crosspicking in an integrated way in their playing. This arrangement of "Wabash Cannonball," represents my effort to play an entire tune in a crosspicked style.

Actually, this arrangement came about as a result of my frustration at not being able to play the tune fingerstyle, like Jerry Reed does on his magnificent rendition. After I listened to Jerry play it, I tried to imitate his fingerstyle arrangement (I'm a closet fingerpicker). But failing that test, I rushed to the assumption that Jerry had overdubbed at least one of the lines (there are **three simultaneous moving parts in his arrangement**). Alas, shortly thereafter, I saw Jerry on television and he played the whole thing live, and with all approriate humility and awe I concluded that I still had quite a few things to learn. Then I arranged the tune for crosspicking.

Let me say at the outset, this is pretty difficult to play. Notice that a crosspicking pattern is only a start; the full arrangement of "Wabash Cannonball" demonstrates that crosspicking is not just **playing patterns,** it's **making music.** And you do that by stretching the pattern or abandoning it altogether when the music (or your taste) might suggest. By the way you can hear this arrangement on the Berline, Crary, and Hickman album, **Night Run** (Sugar Hill) "Wabash Cannonball" is included in a railroad medley, "The BCH Special."

Wabash Cannonball

Traditional, arranged by Dan Crary

Key of G

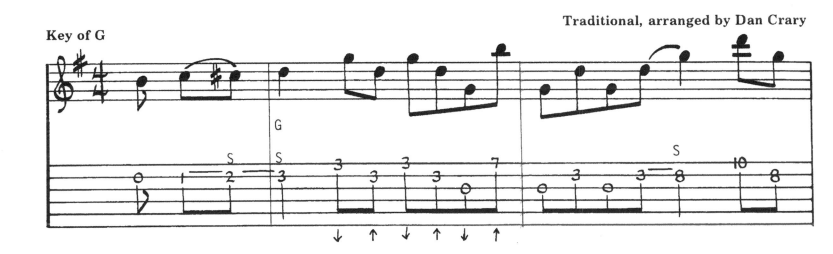

42

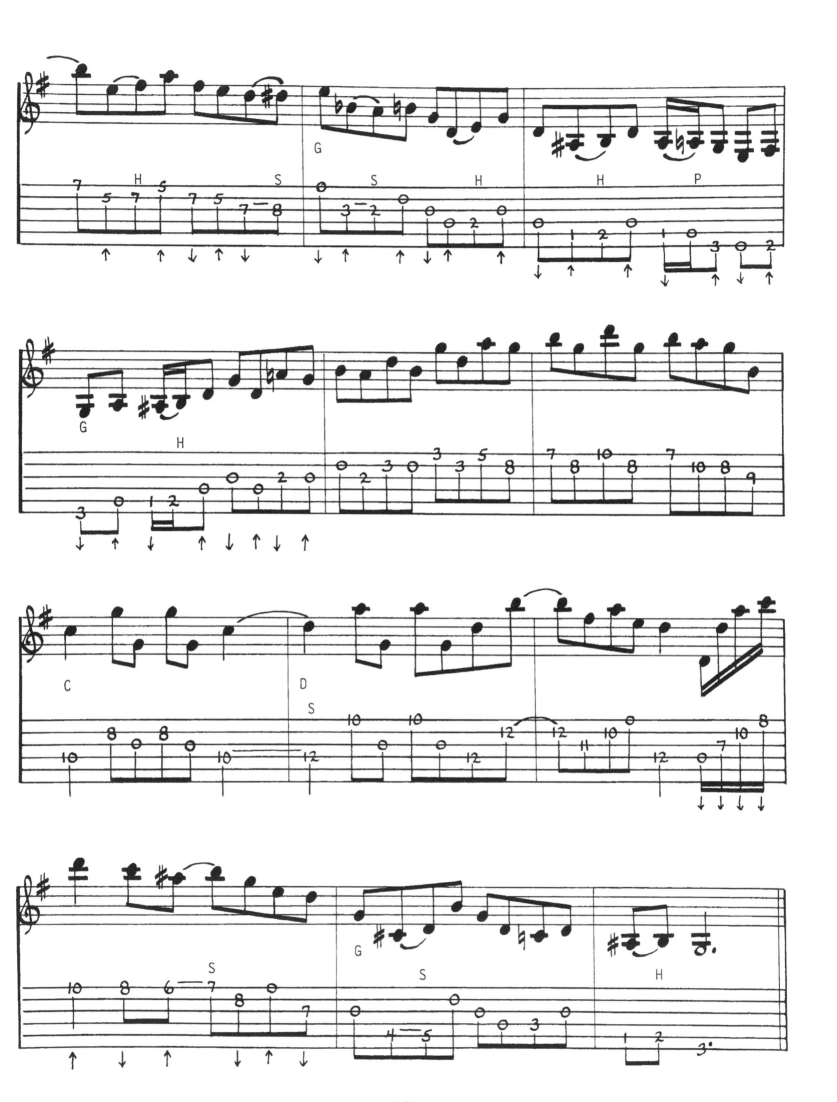

43

Special Guitar Techniques:
LICKS and RUNS

These runs, like everything in this book, are intended to help you make good music on the guitar. I don't think that a few musical tricks or techniques are a substitute for knowing a lot about music and developing taste, finesse, and even restraint where it is needed. But, there is also a place for the flashy in music, and these runs are designed to be both good music and to show off just a little. Actually, showing off is a time-honored part of the performing arts. A great violinist plays a great concerto at least partly to prove that he or she **can** play it, and in the hopes that people will be impressed and moved musically at the same time.

Guitar playing has its flashy, pyrotechnical side too. This section of runs is here, frankly, for ammunition. These licks are meant to attract attention, create power, punctuate, stand out, punch, slash, pound, thrust, and otherwise drive a musical point home. Accordingly, they should be played hard. Some, like the "Cascade" lick, may require a sort of "cross-picked" smoothness of execution, but for the most part these should be given a powerful attack, rather like the **iron fist in the velvet glove.**

After you have learned one of these, what should you do with it? It can be put at the end of a phrase, substituted for an equivalent number of measures in the middle of a tune or break, or otherwise placed in your playing where you can make it fit. One very good use of runs is to provide something predictable and familiar in the middle of a break you have to improvise. Improvisation actually is, in part, the re-use of familiar passages such as these.

First, here are some fairly standard, bluegrassy flatpicking runs.

"G" Runs

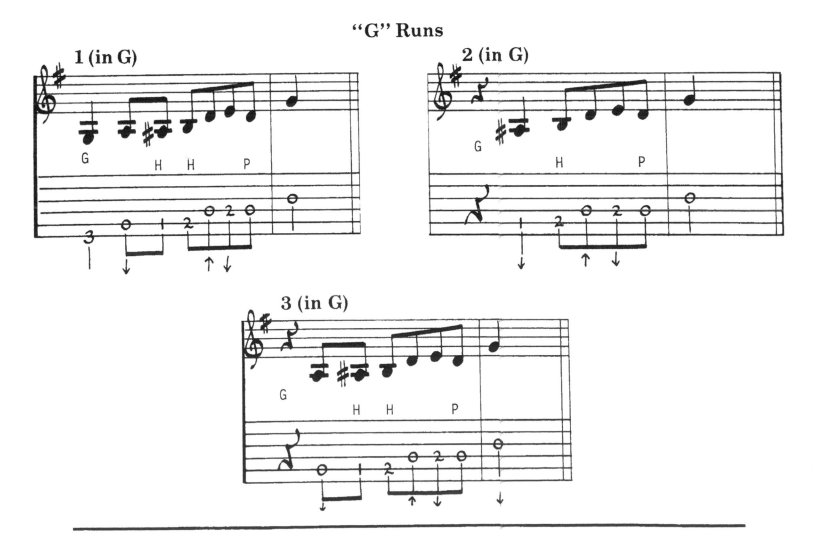

"Treble" Run

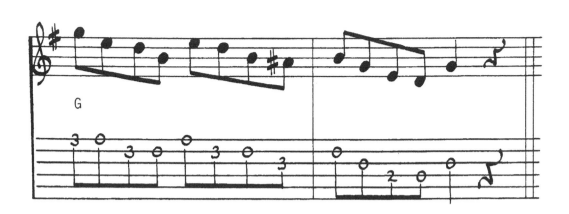

"Golden Era" Run

One of the best sources of ideas for licks and runs are other instruments.
Here are some adapted from banjo and steel guitar.

"Banjo" Runs   1 (in G)

45

2 (in G)

3 (in G)

4 (in D)

"Shot Jackson" Run (in E)

Now, one of my favorites: The "Peaches & Herb" lick is one I heard on that duo's old recording "Love Is Strange". It has a "bluesy" feel that adapts to many different kinds of music.

"Peaches & Herb" Run

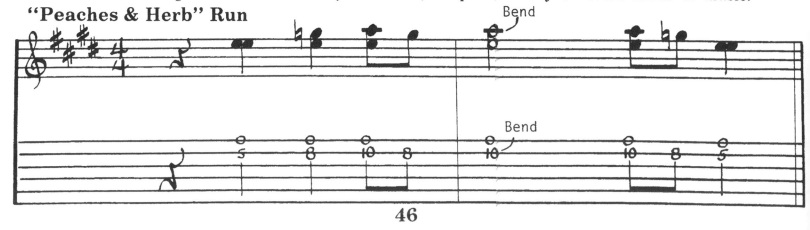

The "Piano Blues" run is one I learned from a piano record twenty-five years ago. Notice that this versatile run is composed of fretted notes, and is therefore easily transposed to any place, any key on the guitar. The bass-string version can be moved down one string (from the fifth, fourth, and third strings to the sixth, fifth, and fourth) using the identical fingerings' in either case, the tonic note is the first note of the run. The idea here is to play a moving bass line against a high drone. Suggested fingerings are provided. Note that you need to deaden the middle string on the third beat of every measure. And everything I have said about the bass string version is true of the treble string version, including that you can move the whole thing down one string, use the same fingering, and you have a transposed run taking its key name from the first note played. **These can be played at any fret, taking their key from the last note of the run.**

"Piano Blues" Run (bass strings)

"Piano Blues" Run (treble strings)

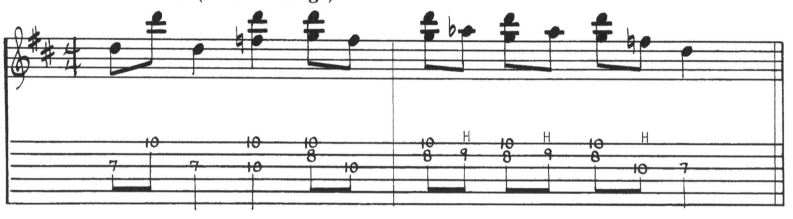

The "Slash" licks (examples A, B & C) are adapted from the paino blues lick in an evolution I discovered about 1965. They should be played hard, making each live up to its name. They work beautifully to punctuate a very fast bluegrass-like passage.

"Slash" Lick (A)

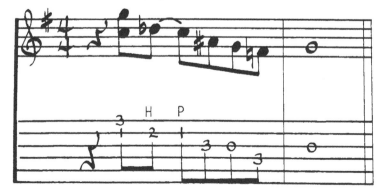

"Slash" Lick (B)   ## "Slash" Lick (C)

The "Floating" run is an easy and impressive-sounding introduction to the technique of playing fretted notes against open-string notes on an adjacent string. To make the run "float", be sure to hold your fingering of the fretted note while you play the next (open) note, so the individual notes overlap.

"Floating" Run

G (Em)

The same principle as above applies to the "Cascade" run. This is a combination of floating and cross-picking techniques. The run was used as part of the introduction to "The Strayaway Child" on my Sugar Hill Record Album, Dan Crary - Guitar (SH 3730). On the recording it is played in the key of E minor, but it works equally well in G major depending on whether you play an E or a G as the final note of the run.

"Cascade" Run

G (Em)

Next, try the "Chain" run below. It is a very easy and bluegrass-like lick that should be used in a fast-tempo break. I played it on the **Guitar** album in the tune "Daybreak In Dixie".

"Chain" Run

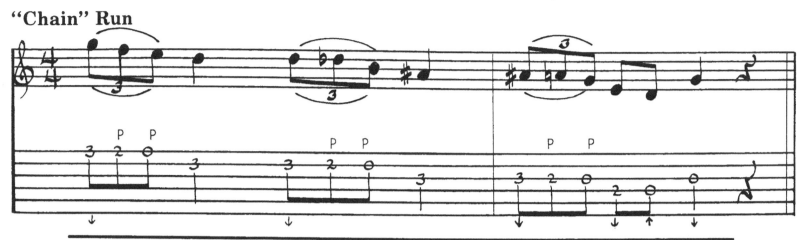

The "Double Stop" run can be used almost anywhere, including as the "two bits" part of a "shave-and-a-haircut" ending.

"Double Stop" Run

Last, let's look at one of the very few runs I've ever borrowed from another guitarist. I'm not against doing that occasionally and I'm always happy to credit the originator of the lick when I do it. In this case, the originator was Clarence White, who used it about twenty years ago as an introduction to a tune. It can be dropped effectively into the middle of a break if you are careful to allocate the necessary number of beats. It's a very tasty, very graceful, bluegrass-type run that will add a little flatpicking "roots" value to your playing.

"Clarence White" Run (1)

"Clarence White" Run (2)

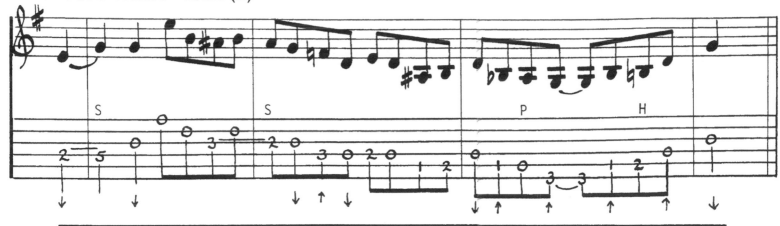

"Floating"

Under the heading of flatpickers-don't-come-up-with-very-classy-names-for-things, "floating" has become a commonly used word to describe the technique of playing fretted strings next to open strings in such a way as to create a "loud pedal" or sustained effect that occurs when each note is held a bit longer than it normally would be, making it sustain into the next note and overlap. The section on runs demonstrates this with the "floating" lick and the "cascade" lick. In the following short arrangement of Gold Rush by Bill Monroe (with some help from Byron Berline) the technique is embedded in a tune. Be sure to let the notes in the sections marked "float" overlap so the effect is clearly there. You might want to try the runs before tackling the tune. Then when you see how it works from these examples, look for your own ideas in the technique: a good place to look is around the 7th and 8th frets of the second, third, and fourth strings; these strings at those frets are a step or a step-and-a-half above the next higher string played open; playing the two notes in close proximity creates the floating effect (sounds a little like Isodora Duncan on the Guitar), if you can find spots where those notes fit a break or tune, you can apply the technique elsewhere.

Gold Rush

Key of A

By Bill Monroe

Part 1

Repertoire Building

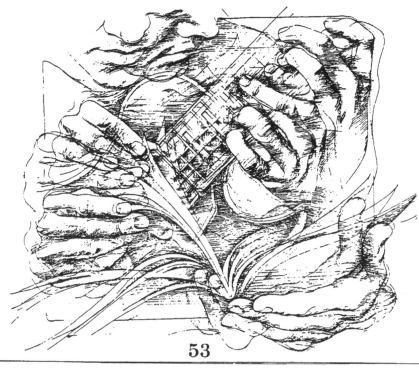

NOTE: Due to time limitations the songs "Memories of Mozart" and "Sweet Laree" are not on the cassette.

Flop-Eared Mule

Key of D
Position: OPEN

Traditional, arranged by Dan Crary

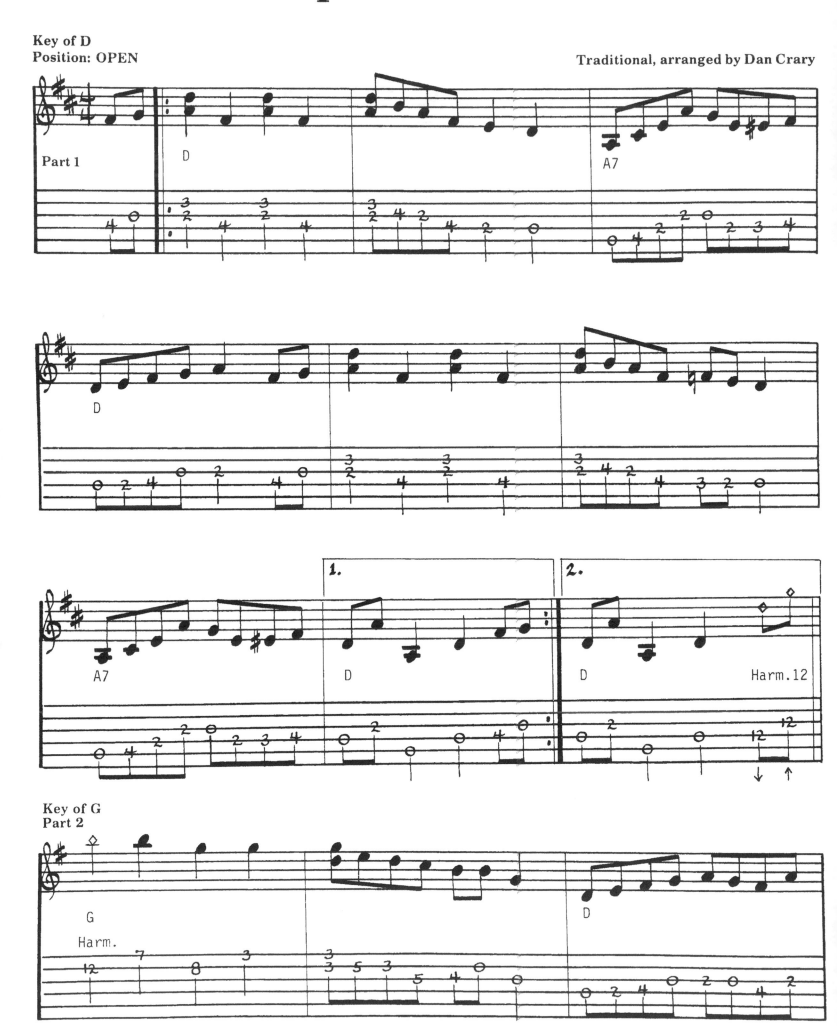

Ragtime Annie

Key of D
Capo, 2nd Fret

Traditional, arranged by Dan Crary

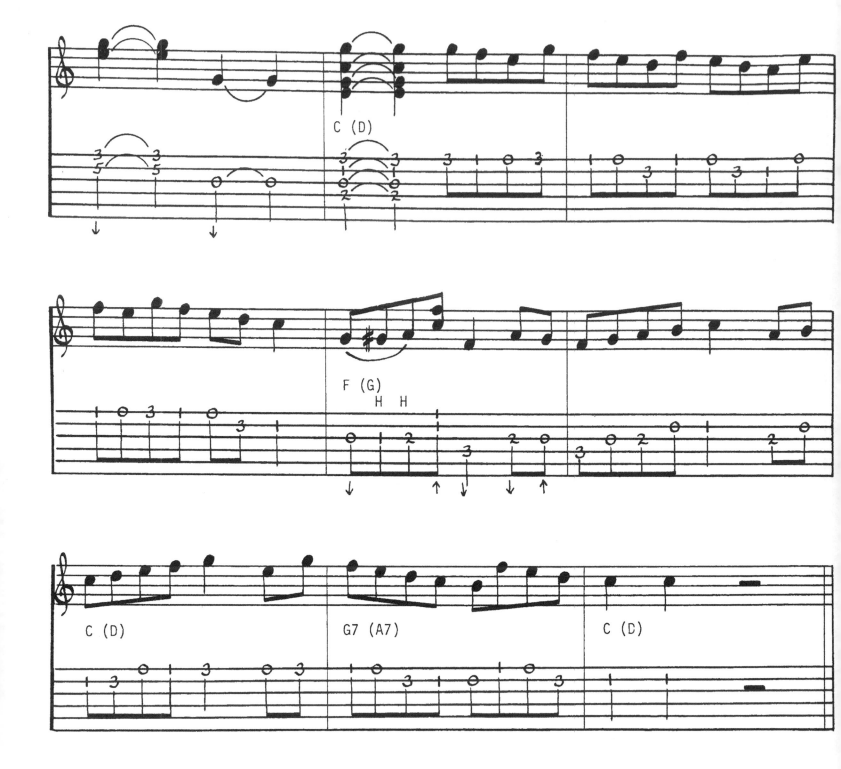

Berline • Crary • Hickman

Red Haired Boy
(Duet)

Key of A
Capo, 2nd fret

Traditional, arranged by Dan Crary

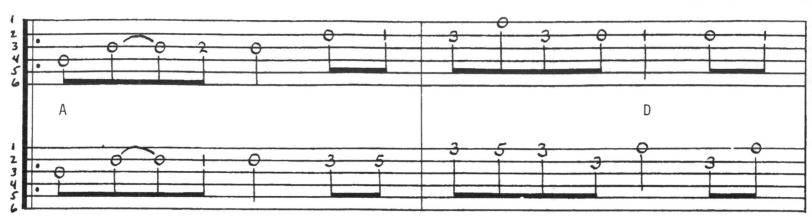

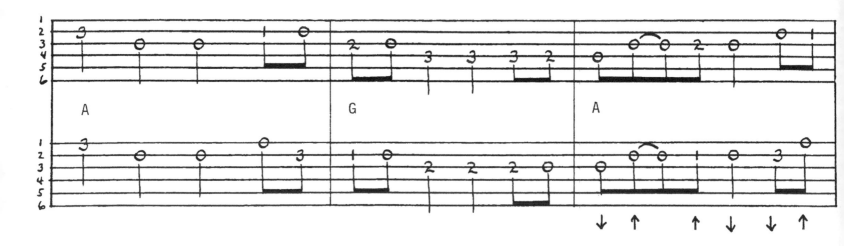

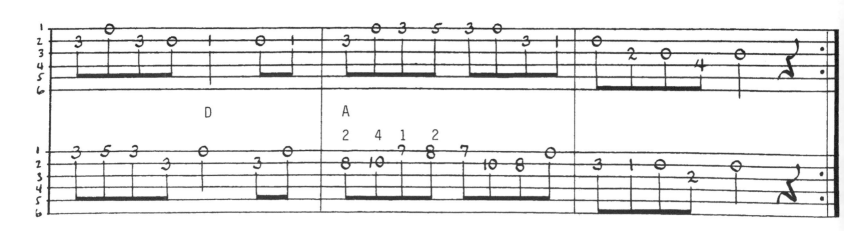

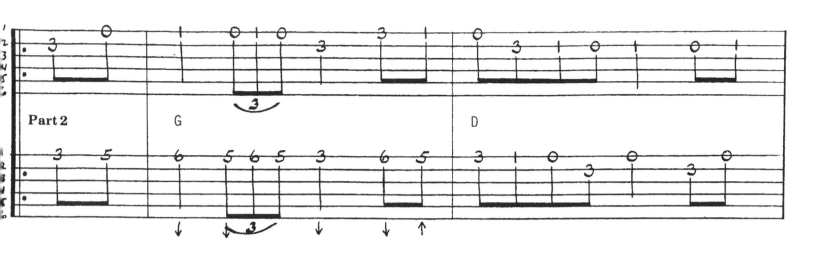

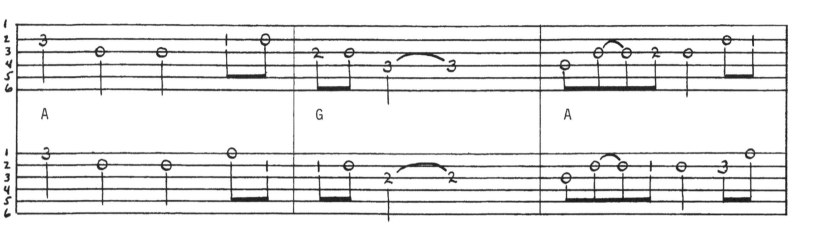

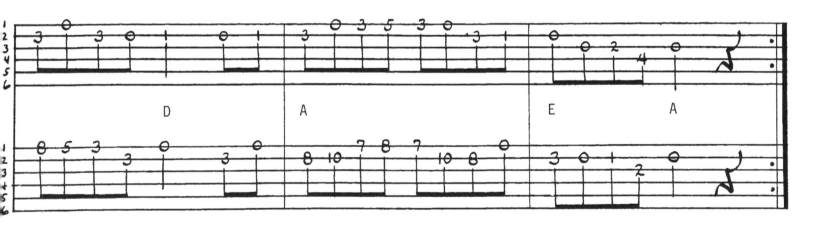

Reuben

Key of D
Position: OPEN
Tuning: Drop D

Traditional, arranged by Dan Crary

Part 3

Done Gone

Key of G (Bb)
Capo, 3rd fret

Traditional, arranged by Dan Crary

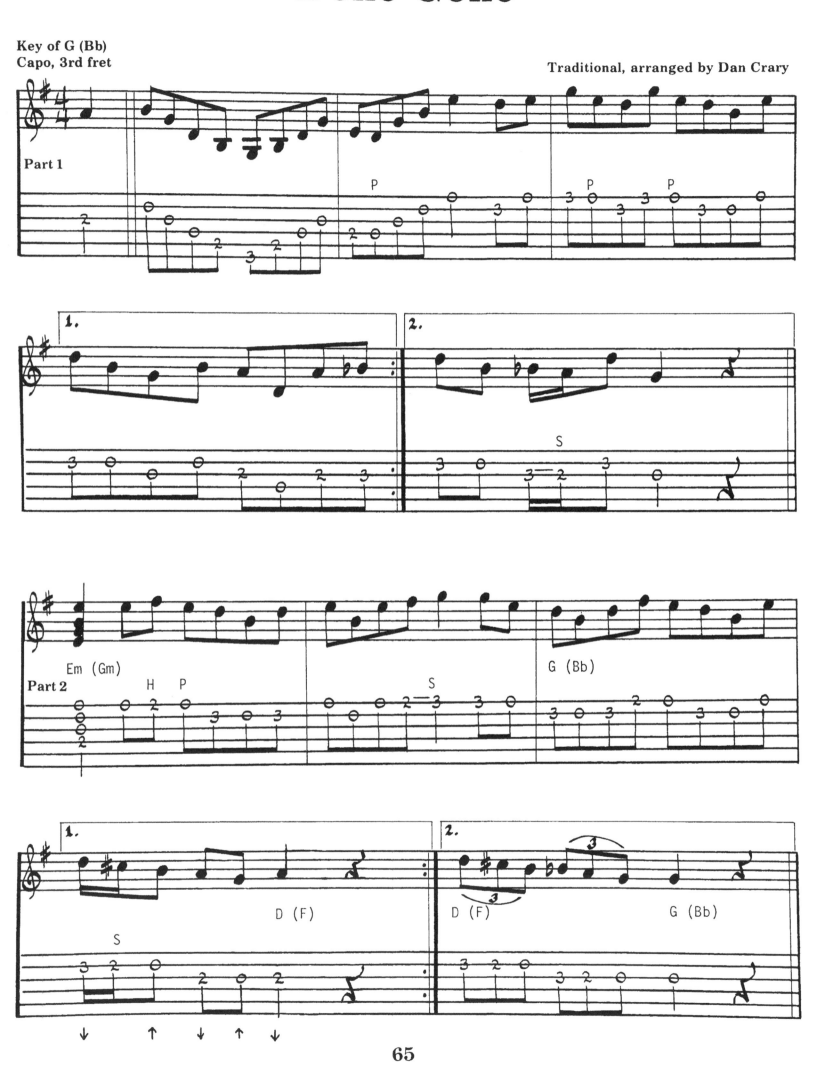

Dill Pickle Rag

Key of C

Traditional, arranged by Dan Crary

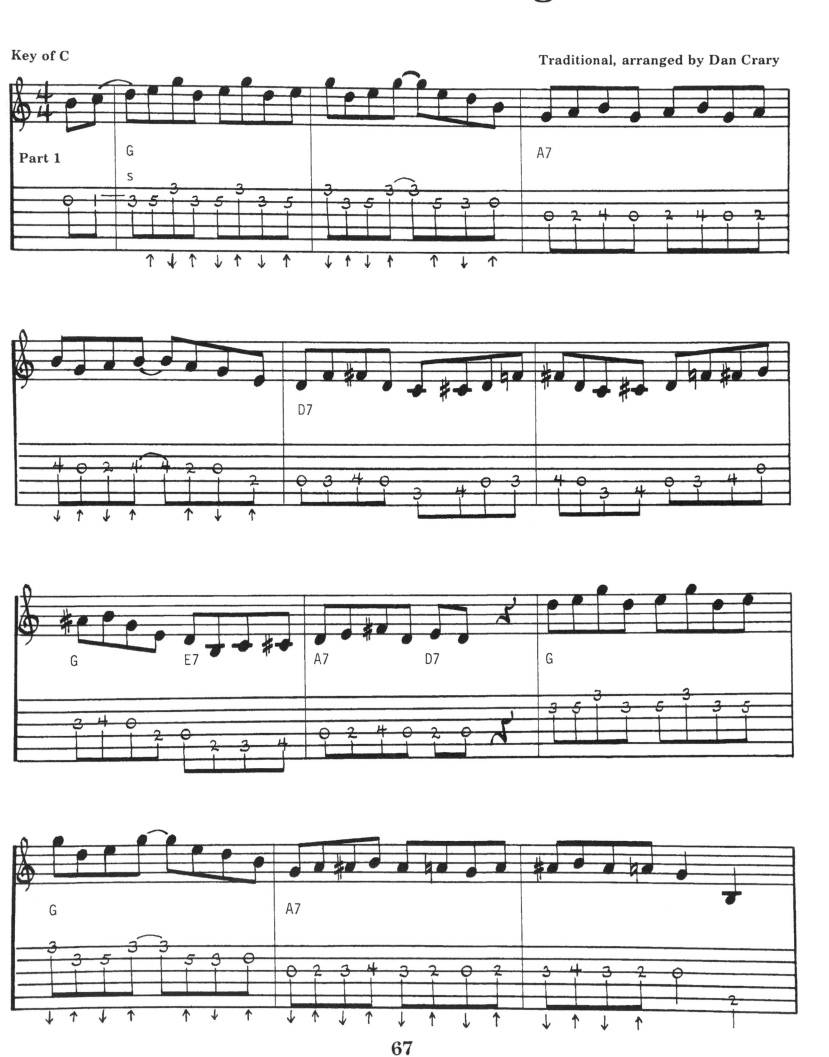

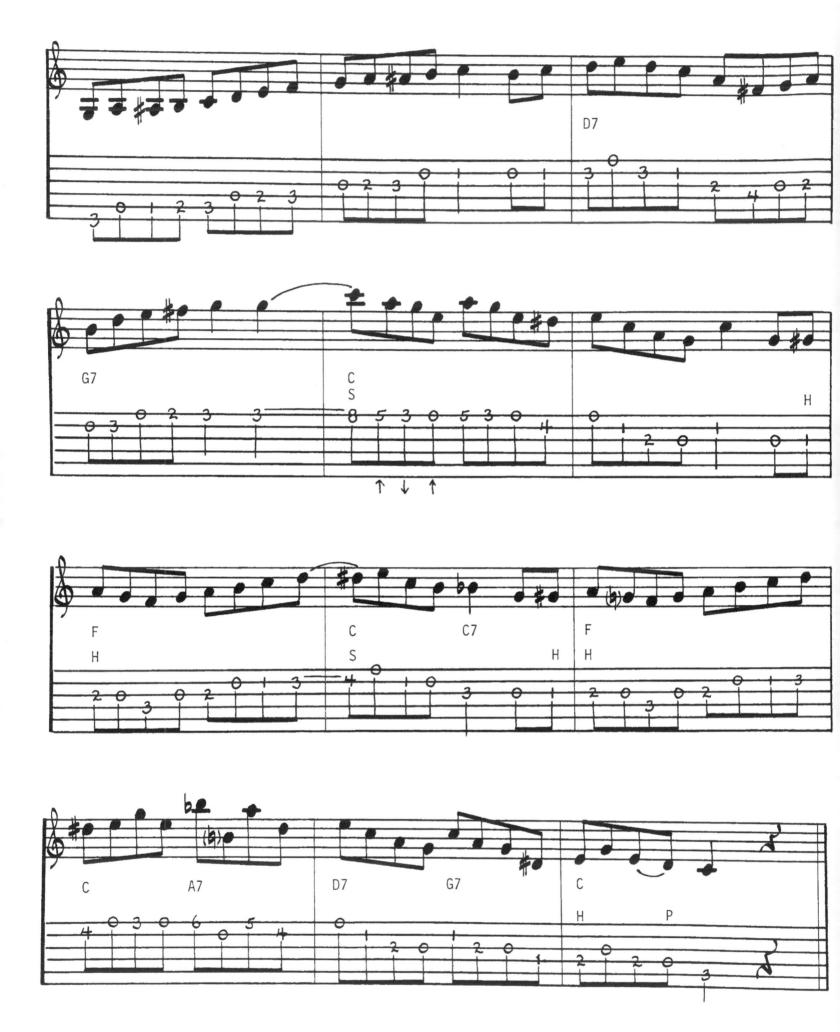

Blackberry Blossom

Key of G

Traditional, arranged by Dan Crary

Second Version
Part 1

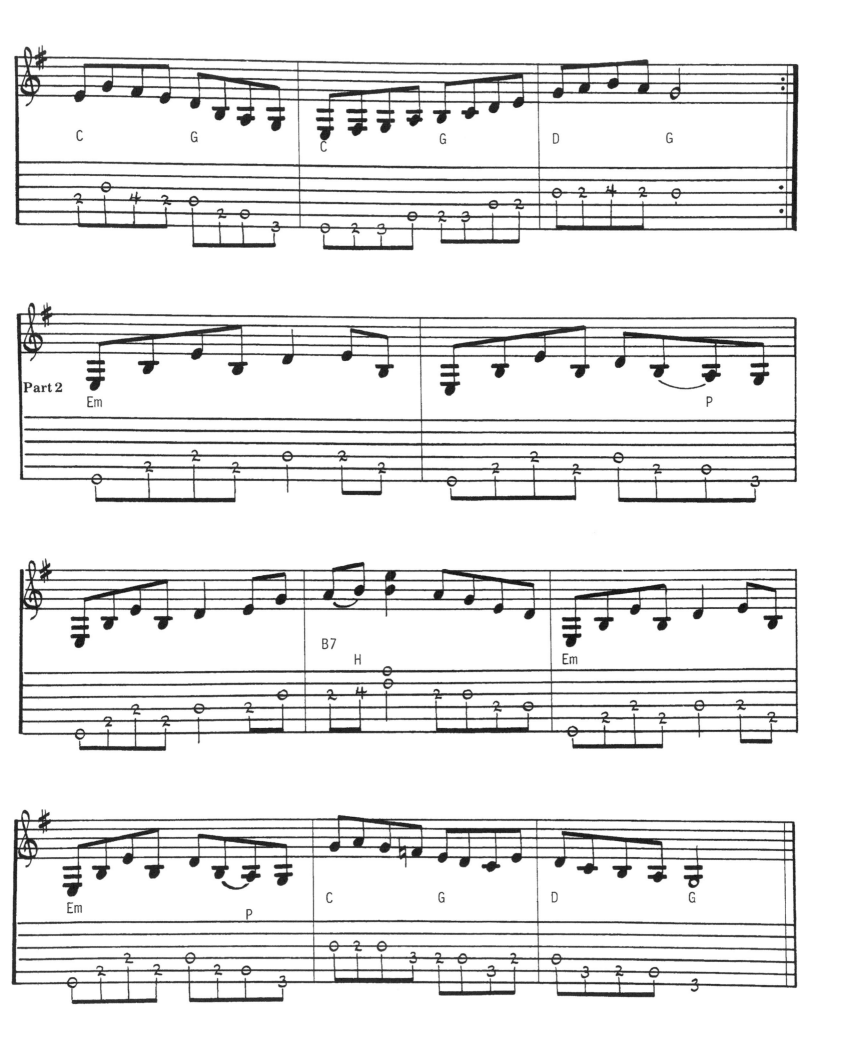

Lady's Fancy

Key of G
Intro: Rubato

Traditional, arranged by Dan Crary

Part 5

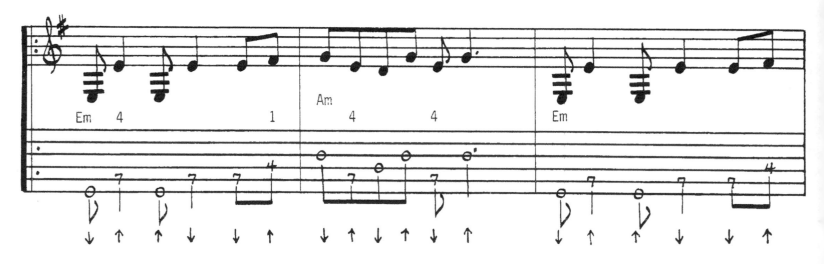

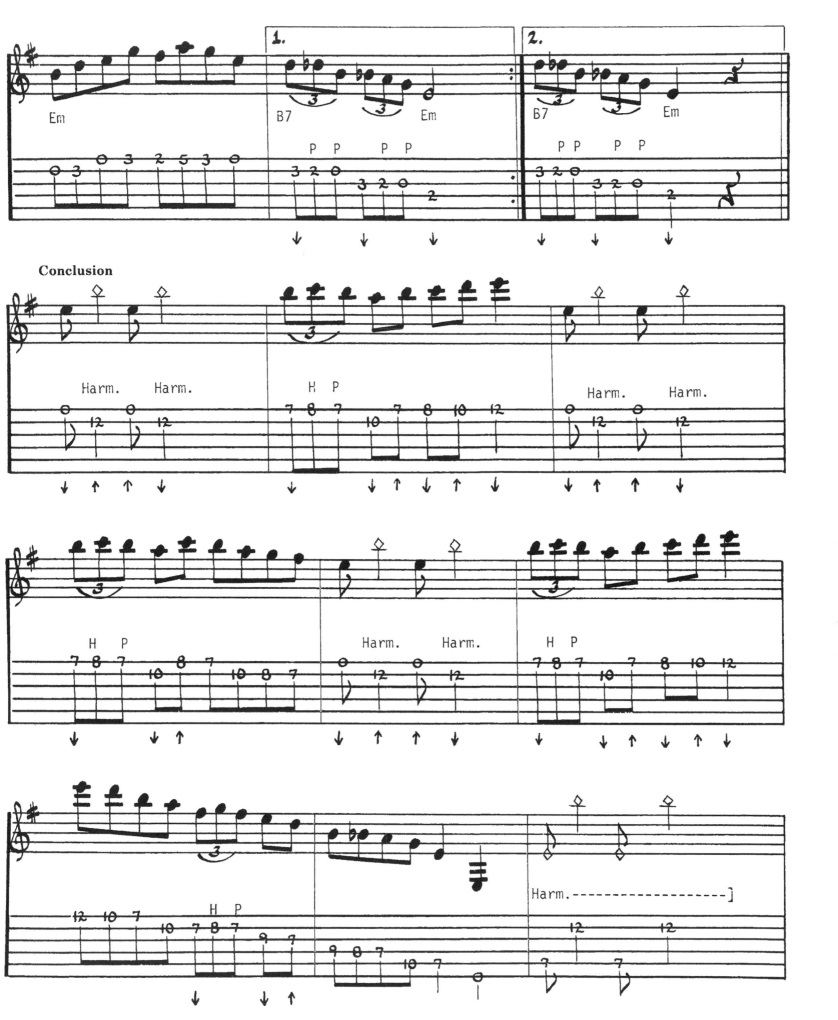

Conclusion

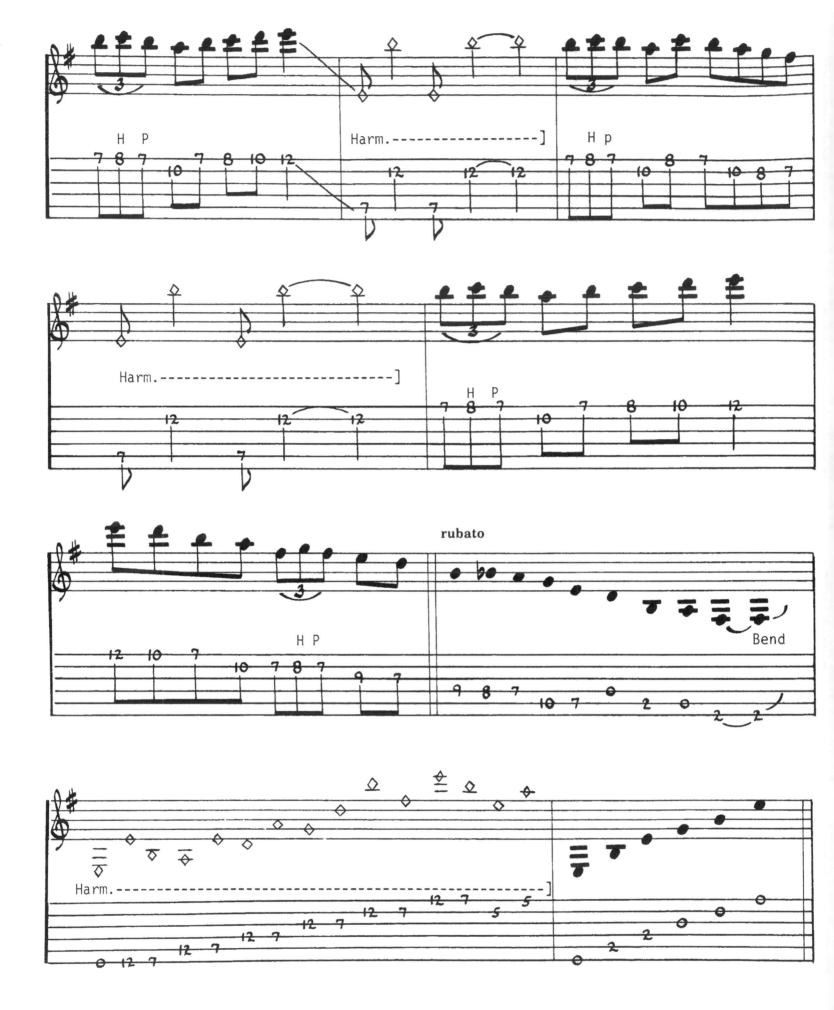

The Dusty Miller

Traditional, arranged by Dan Crary

Key of A
Capo 2nd Fret

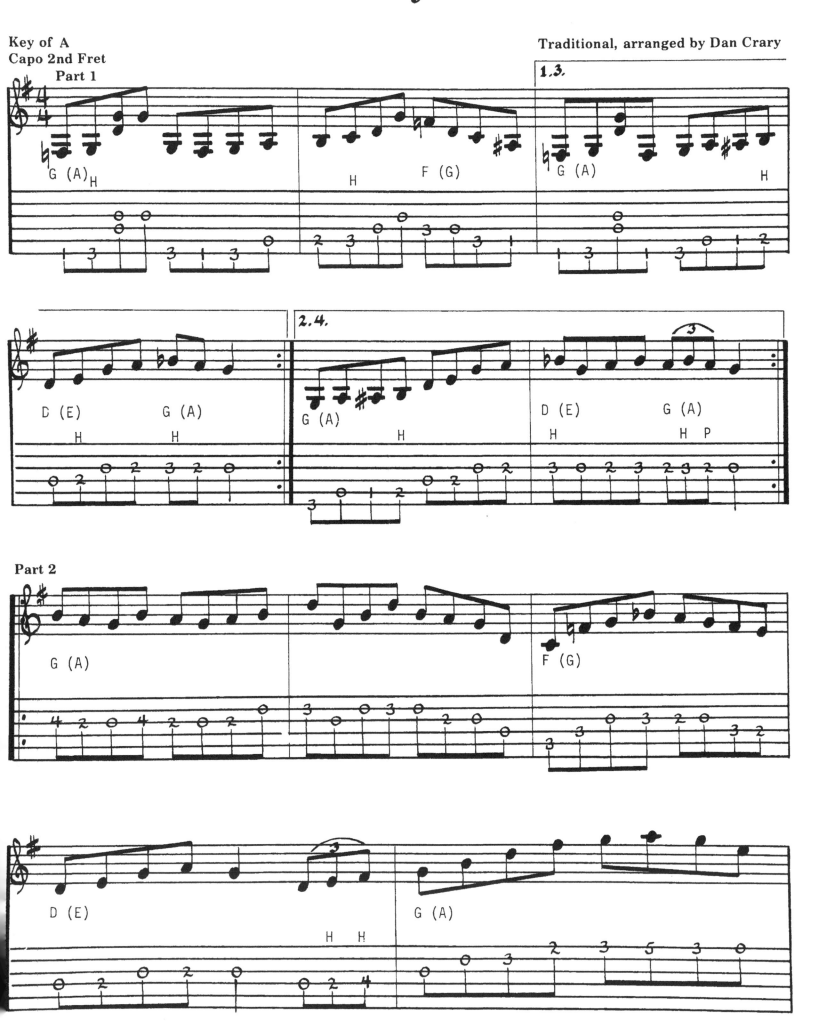

Part 3

Part 4

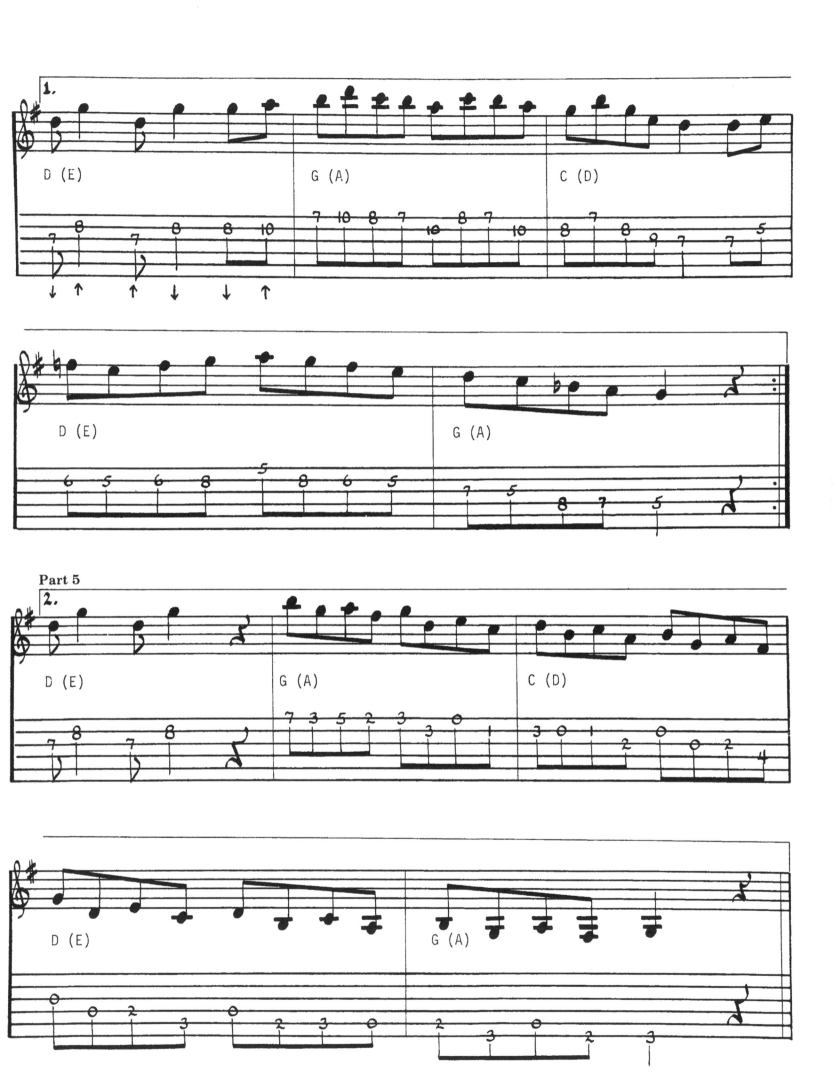

Part 5

83

Lime Rock

Key of E

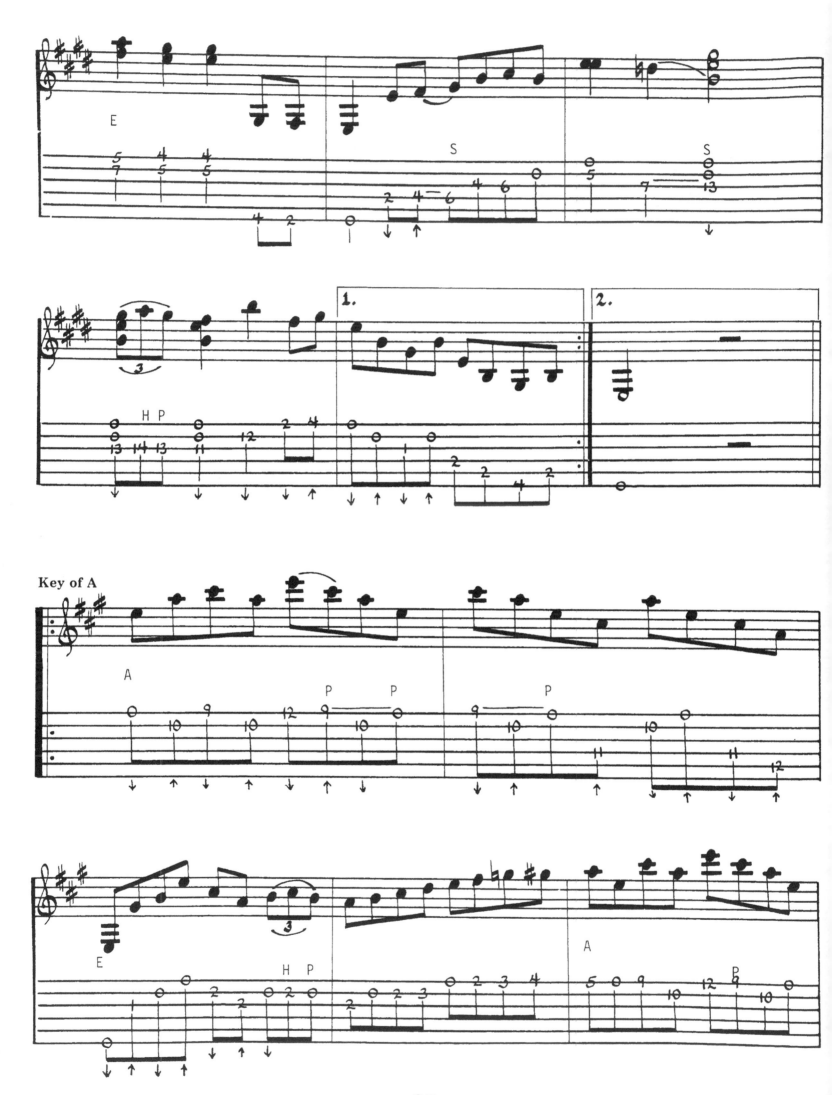

Key of D

Key of A

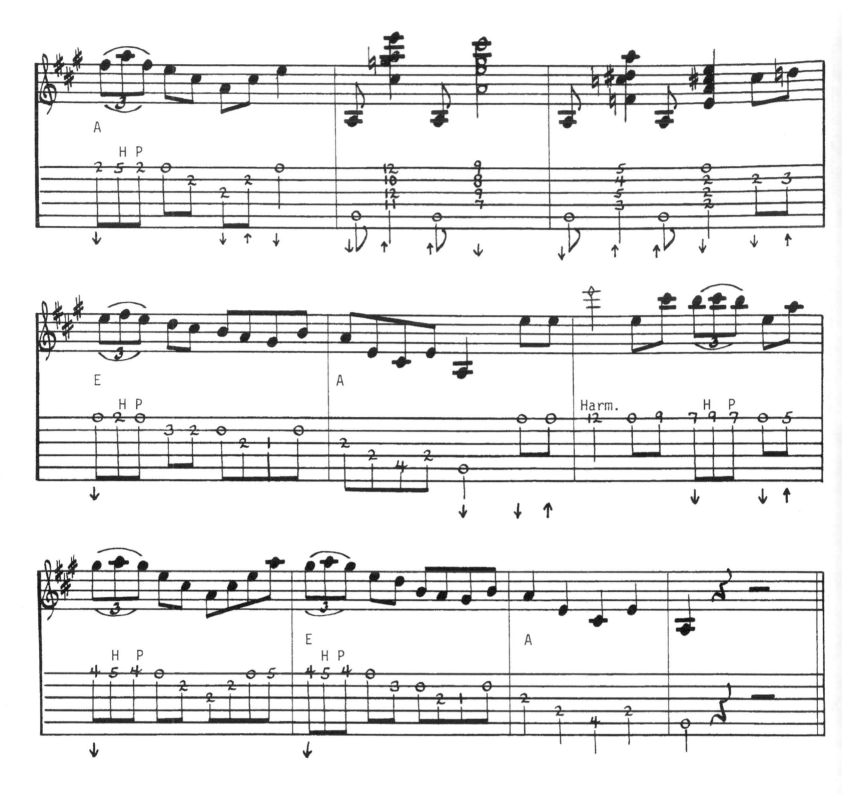

Huckleberry Hornpipe

Key of A
Capo 2nd Fret

By Byron Berline
Arranged by Dan Crary

Part 1

Part 3

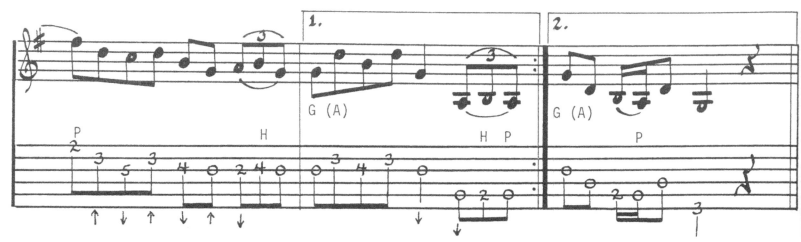

Memories of Mozart

Key of Am
Position: OPEN

Traditional, arranged by Dan Crary

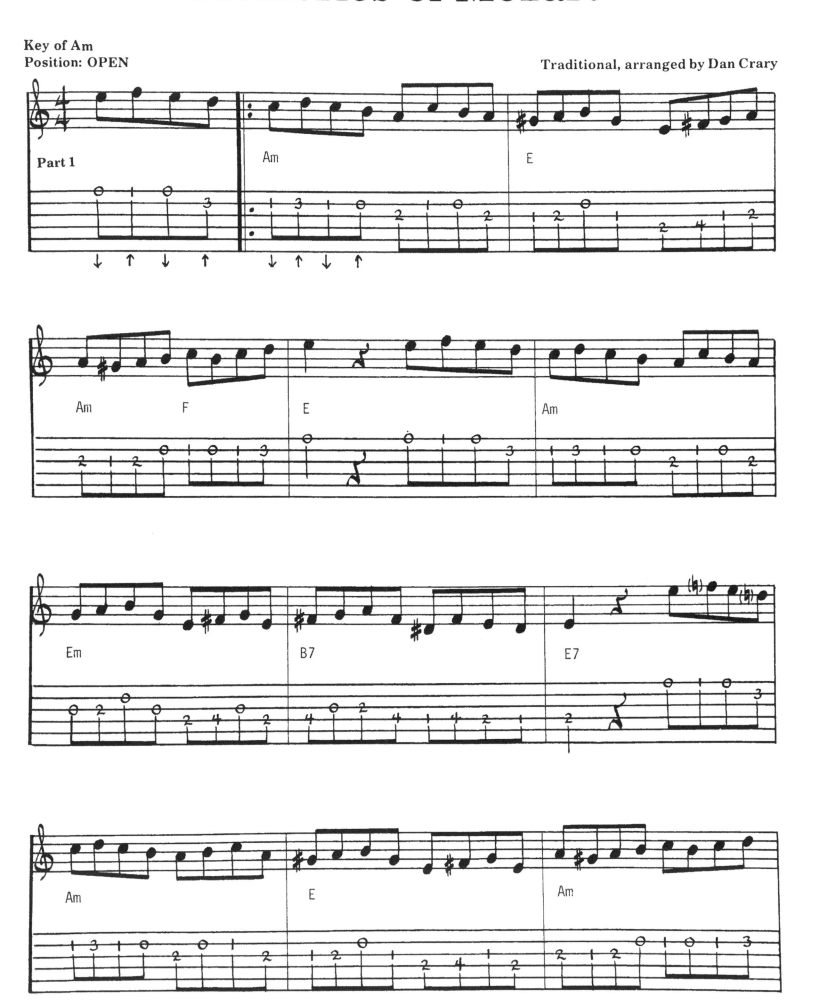

Part 4

Sweet Laree

Key of E
Position: OPEN

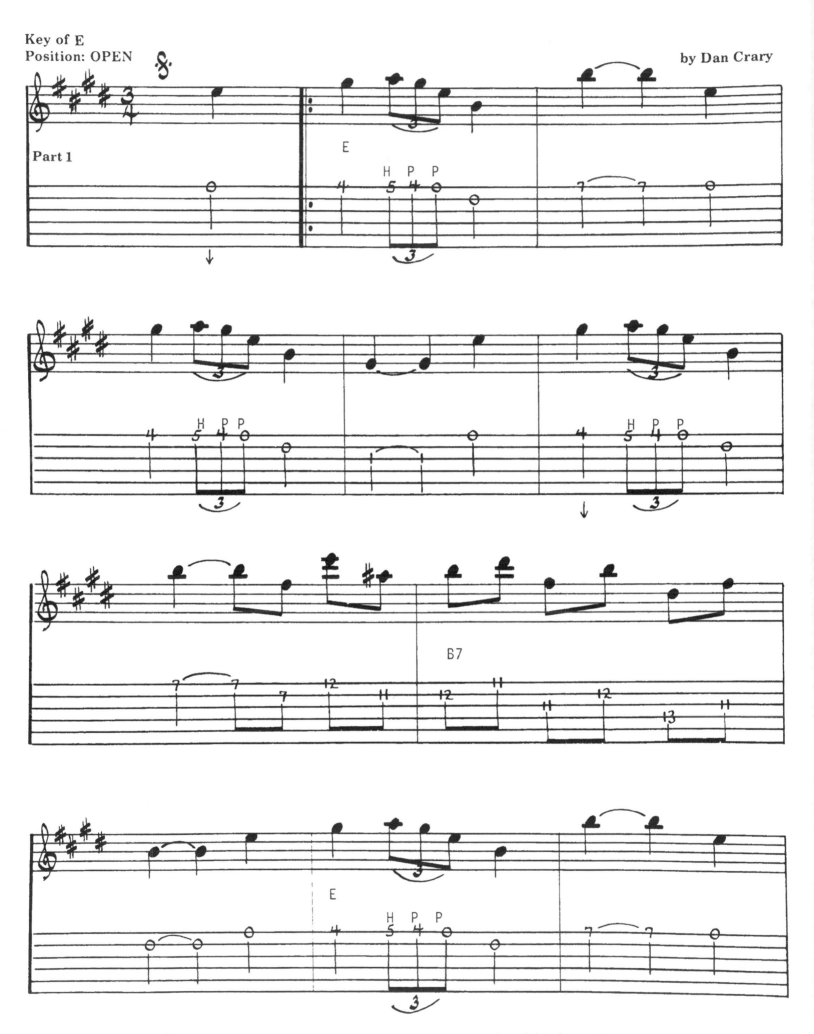

by Dan Crary

Part 1

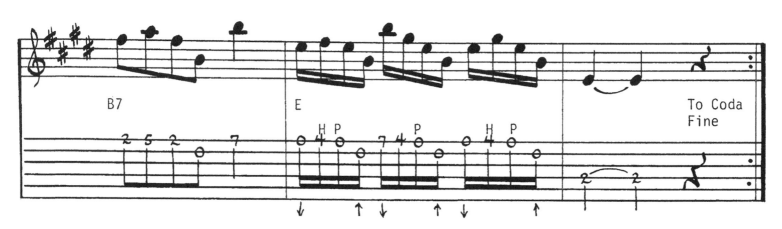

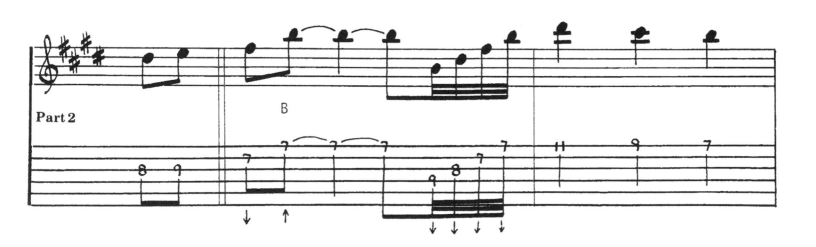

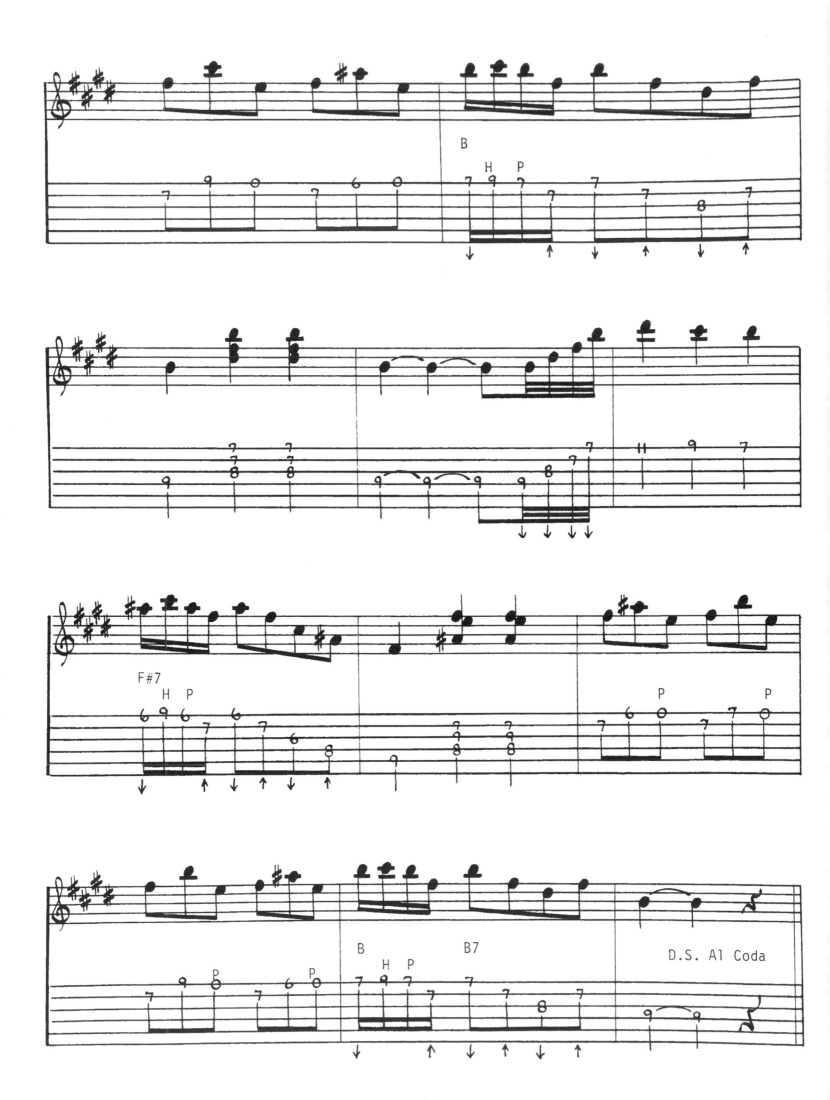

coda

Part 3

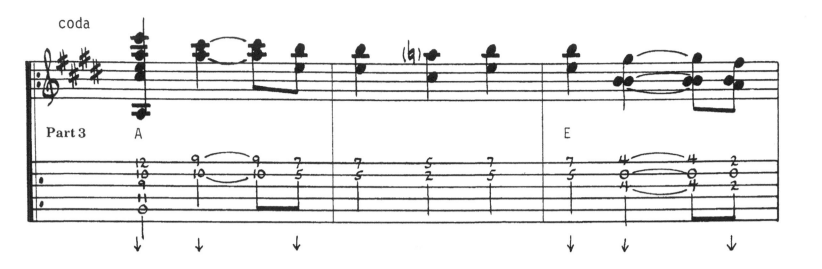

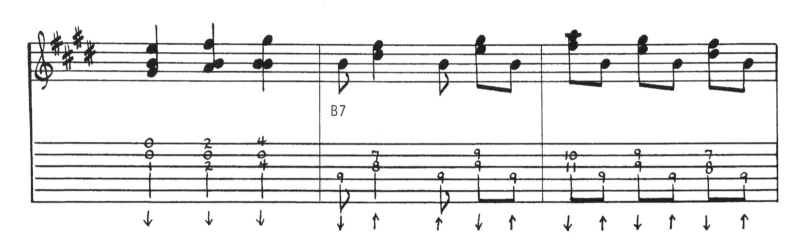

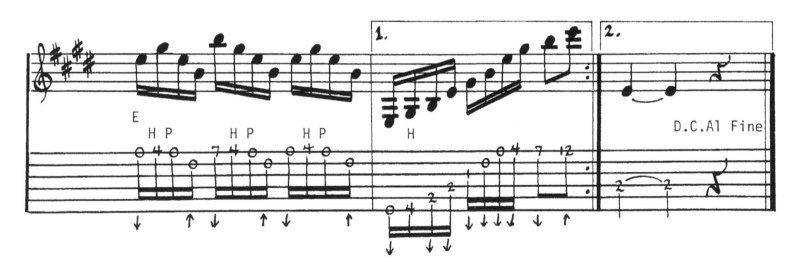

═══ A selected Dan Crary discography ═══

● **Dan Crary solo albums**
   Ladys Fancy-Rounder records #0099
   Sweet Southern Girl-Sugar Hill #3707
   Dan Crary/Guitar-Sugar Hill #3730
   Take A Step Over-Sugar Hill #3755

● **Berline, Crary & Hickman**
   Night Run-Sugar Hill #3729
   Berline, Crary & Hickman-Sugar Hill #3720
   B.C.H.-Sugar Hill #3770

Learning Tunes
From The Original Instruments

Learning a fiddle tune from a fiddle player is something you should do for yourself at least once. It will amaze you to discover the little inside things that an instrumentalist does which add up to that break or version that sounds so fine in a performance or recording. The trick in doing this, at least for me, is to slow down what is happening so it comes across in understandable slow motion. I use a two-speed tape recorder (cassette and reel types are available), record the fiddle version at the fast speed, then play it back at the slow speed. Because the slow speed on these machines is exactly half the fast speed, three handy things happen:

1. The tune is slower by half.
2. The pitch is lowered into the same pitch range as the guitar.
3. The key is the same.

Then listen to the tune a few times to get a feel for the "forest". After that, go through the tune phrase by phrase to get a listen to the "trees". My approach is to listen to each phrase or short section until I can hum or whistle it, then (and **only** then) I find it on the guitar. When I've dragged myself through one whole part of the tune and learned it exactly as the fiddler played it, I run over it a few times and put what I've learned down on a separate tape. That way, as I go on to the next section I won't forget my new-found information from the preceding part.

This can be a time-comsuming and laborious process, but the rewards are stupendous. The first time I did this on a tune that I had played for several years but not learned right, it was a real eye-opener. I found that there was a lot more going on than my guitar-player's ears had picked up, until I slowed the thing down.

The ultimate goal is this: **when you know exactly how the fiddler played the tune, then move on to alter the tune a little to make it sound like guitar music. Create an arrangement. But the arrangement you come up with will be VASTLY different from the one you would have faked your way into with just a vague inpression of the tune. Learning a piece this way has the added advantage of educating your musical sense. . .music is self-teaching in** this sense: the more music you learn **right** the more **musical** you will become in everything you do.

Approaches
To Right Hand Position

There are so many different approaches to how to position the right hand in flatpicking, somebody could write a book about that alone. It wouldn't be a very useful book, however, because no one really knows whether there is one best way or not. What I will describe here is an approach that works for me: in addition it has worked well for several people who tried this approach because their own version was not working well. Rather than tell you to use my approach, I'd recommend that you position your right hand in such a way as to meet a few guidelines, whether it's my own hand position or not.

GUIDELINES FOR YOUR RIGHT HAND:

1. The right hand should be in the same position each time you play: some players never get in practice because things never feel the same due to a shifting hand position. Don't re-invent the guitar every time you play. . .find a good position and stay with it. With experience, you may then shift around to vary the tone of the passage you're playing, but when learning, one basic position needs to feel familiar. The goal is to be able to watch the left hand while you play; the right hand should become so familiar with the territory, you seldom have to look at it.

2. The right hand position should leave the hand free to move across the strings. Avoid a position that makes you push hard against the position itself; the pick needs to move rapidly and freely across the strings. On the other hand, too much freedom can be undesireable; consider point 3.

3. The right hand position should provide maximum control; it's a point with several aspects:

   a. The right hand should move as little as possible to get the job done. Wasted motion results in lost precision, and mistakes.

   b. The right hand (for most players) should rest on the bridge or on the top of the guitar. Because flatpicking necessitates playing both loud and fast on occasion, most players find that the free-floating approach doesn't provide sufficiently solid control.

4. The right hand position should be the one which works for you. If yours is working well for you, don't mess up a good thing. It's possible to become so worried about finding the best right hand position that you never get around to playing. The best position is one that is comfortable, works, and makes it possible not to think about it all the time.

5. If you decide to change your approach to positioning the right hand, decide on an approach, then change cold turkey. One of the worst things to do is to change back and forth, sit on the fence, never give the new position a chance to feel right. It takes a couple of weeks or more for a new hand position to become familiar. To sum up, don't change unnecessarily, but if necessary, make a change that meets the above criteria, and make it completely.

MY APPROACH TO POSITIONING THE RIGHT HAND

As you can see in the accompanying photograph, I rest my wrist on the bridge. Actually, it's a little bone at the bottom of the wrist which rests at the fourth string bridge pin. From this position the right hand **pivots** so the pick can reach from the sixth to the first string. At first glance it looks a little strange, but then almost any right hand position anybody uses looks awkward. If you need to change your present approach, I recommend this one because it meets the criteria I've outlined above. Among those who have adopted this method, I can report about an 80% success rate. But nothing works the same for everyone: whether you use this approach, modify it, or do something different, remember the goal is to settle on one, then get on with learning to **play!**

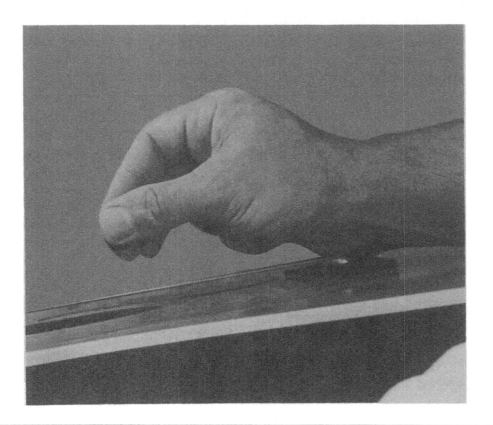

Holding The Pick

How you hold the pick is another one of those nobody-agrees-on-it questions. The traditional way of holding the pick looks like this:

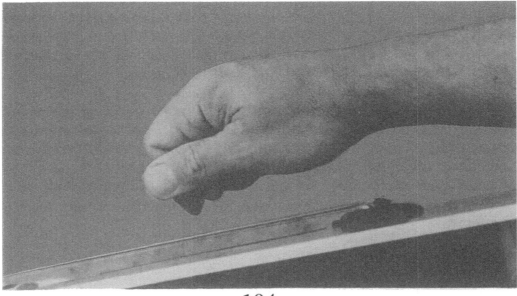

I started out this way when I started the guitar. But because of the need for greater control and a stronger basic position, I gradually came around to my present approach which looks like this:

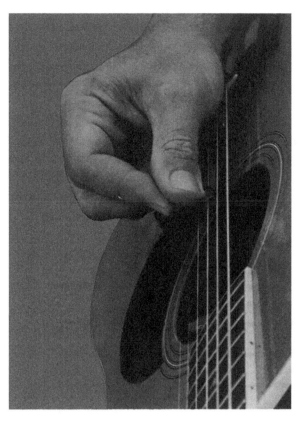 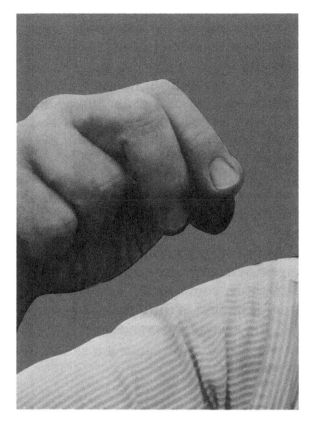

Let me point out a couple of things about this approach:

First, it seems to fit well with the hand position I've discussed in the previous section.

Second, the feature of thumb on one side, tips of two fingers on the other gives greater strength, prevents pick rotation, and leaves only two other fingers to keep out of the way.

Third, notice that the part of the pick which strikes the strings is more **round** than **pointed.** The rounded corner of a pick seems to provide a "fatter" tone on treble strings, and it's easier for me to control on fast passages than the point.

I would suggest that you experiment with the difference yourself. Start with a medium gauge pick about this shape and size:

Try playing with the point, then compare that to the rounded corner, and notice the difference in the sound produced. Then try some different guages, and so on. One other note: picks with smooth, polished edges will make less extraneous pick noies than picks which come out of the mold with rough edges.

LEFT HAND VARIATIONS
CHORDS

In this section I want to introduce you briefly to the subject of variations in chords. Since it's an introduction only, we'll look at ways to vary chords of the open position, primarily. I hope someday you'll get interested in a serious study of music and guitar theory that will take you further into the fascinating world of chords. But you don't have to do that to discover some easy and beautiful changes you can make in standard chord fingerings. These changes will do a lot to vary the sound of your music and make your job as an accompanist more rewarding and interesting.

First, notice as you finger any major chord that there are only three different notes in each one. You may use all six strings, but there will be some duplication of musical notes to spread the three across all six strings. Take the "G" chord; if you check, you'll see that there are G, B, and D notes only. In fact, the formal definition of a G major chord would be the first (G), third (B), and Fifth (D) notes of the G scale. All major chords consists of the first, third, and fifth notes of it's major scale. Funny thing, a lot of flatpickers "sort of" know that, but no one has ever told them why it's useful to know.

Well, here's why: you can change the sound and the effect or "feel" of a chord by making simple changes in the way those three notes are arranged. For example, compare the sounds of these two G chords. The first is the standard, open position G chord, the second is a variation.

variation 1

Clearly, both are G chords, but there's a difference. How would you describe the difference? Is the first "warmer"? Is the second "harder" or "colder" or more piercing? Which word you choose doesn't matter; what counts is that you hear the difference. Try to imagine some places where one might sound better than the other. Try playing the "softer" sounding chord during a quiet passage of a tune, then shift to the "harder" version during a loud or driving passage. You and I might not make the shift at the same place, but that would be OK. What I want you to see is the possibility that by changing wherever your musical sense tells you to, you create variety, a different mood, a different dynamic.

WHY DO THESE CHORDS SOUND DIFFERENT?

It's because of what is called "voicing" of chords. This has to do with how often a particular note appears in the chord and in which order. In our example, we make the second chord sound harsh or hard by leaving out all the B notes or thirds, and adding a D or fifth to the chord. In other words, you can change the effect of a chord by adding or subtracting thirds or fifths. Even if you don't know a lot about music, you can begin to figure out what the thirds and fifths of open position major chords are just by watching what notes are occurring in these familiar chords patterns. Or, check this chart and experiment with ways to add or subtract thirds and fifths from various chords.

Chord	A	B	C	D	E	F	G
Scale:							
First or "1"	A	B	C	D	E	F	G
Third or "3"	C#	D#	E	F#	G#	A	B
Fifth or "5"	E	F#	G	A	B	C	D

Here's an example, we see in the chart that with a D chord, the third is an F# and the fifth is an A. First, let's "soften" or "warm up" the D chord by adding more thirds or F#'s.

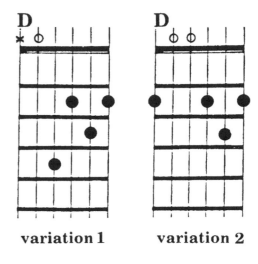

variation 1   variation 2

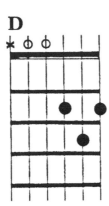

D

In the first variation we added an F# on the forth string; in the second, we added it on the sixth string. Hear the change? Now, let's try "hardening" the basic D chord by adding a fifth or A note. About the only way to do that in the open position is shown in the example.

Note that as we added the A or fifth, we also got rid of an F# or third, so the effect is to make the chord much harsher or "harder".

The following chords are a partial list of variations in open position chords for you to try and experiment with. I urge you to find some of your own and think about where it might enhance your music to use them. In addition, I've included just a few other kinds of chord vaiations that work in the open position and might be useful to you on occasion. But again, a caution: The straighter a traditional tune or song, the less you may want to change the chord structure, some kinds of music may not be sutable places for chords like 9ths or other more "modern" sounding variations. when in doubt, "play it like it was wrote". . . let the music itself speak to you about where a variation might be good **and** about where it wouldn't.

Chord Chart

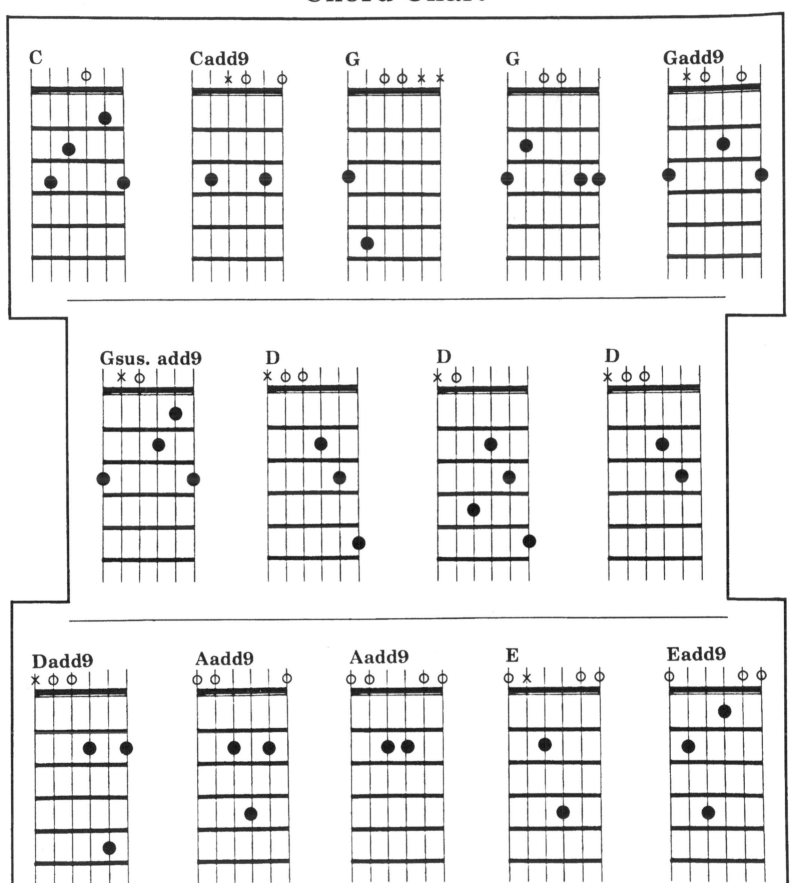

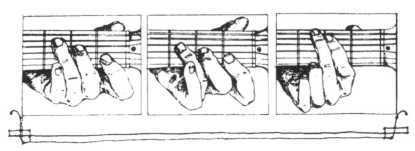

Your Guitar

Most flatpicking is done on a large-body steel string guitar. Almost any acoustic guitar can be flatpicked, but the style seems to fit the big-bodied, "dreadnaught" shaped guitar using medium guage or light medium strings. If your guitar differs from that description, don't despair; the typical flatpicker's guitar is best for performing, but you can certainly go a long way toward learning the style playing any playable acoustic guitar. I would recommend that at such a time as you decide to acquire another instrument in the future, that you consider carefully a steel-string model with a fairly large body so that the techniques and repertoire you learn in these pages will give you the most satisfying results. Almost all acoustic guitar makers make a "drednaught" shaped insrument. The Martin Company (who invented the shape in 1934) still offers a complete line. In addition several established independents make fine instruments, often with the advice of an established performer. Some of my own preferences are embodied in the Dan Crary model guitar made by Taylor Guitars.

Steps to follow in selecting a guitar

- Play a **lot** of different instruments. Find a retailer who offers several different models and compare them side-by-side.
- Be sure to check not only the standard brands, but the smaller companies and independent luthiers (guitar makers) as well. Some of the greatest guitars ever made are being made today, both in factories and in small shops.
- Get lots of advice, then take it with a couple grains of salt. Guitar players are famous for having opinions about instruments, but not necessarily for being objective about them. If you can find someone who is unbiased and knowledgeable (good luck!) consider his or her ideas as part of your information gathering process.
- Here's a **good** tip: find a couple of **good** instrument repair persons with experience repairing and adjusting several makes. Get their opinion about the reliability and repairability of the various makes. All good quality guitars need periodic adjustment, accidents do happen, frets wear out, and so on. . .knowing a good repair person will be important to you in the future.

Criteria for judging a guitar

- The first and most important criterion is **Sound**. The bass register should be solid and loud, but clear. The treble should also be loud and clear with what is called "sustain" (treble and bass notes should continue to sound a few seconds after being played). The most common problems of sound are either too much bass coupled with a weak treble response and little sustain, or lots of sustain coupled with a thin treble and a bass sound that seems restricted. One thing to try is playing treble and bass strings softly, then harder and harder. A well-balanced guitar should increase in volume as it is played harder although some instruments do not. Another good idea, have somebody whose judgement you trust come along to listen as you play and play as you listen from across a room and/or over a PA system.
- A second criterion is structural soundness. Seek expert advice on this one (see # 4 above). Find out about a company's or maker's reputation for reliability.
- Money is, of course an issue. Only you can decide how much you can afford, and because prices vary over time, I can't tell you how much to spend. One standard warning is that good guitars don't come cheap. True, in a sense. But I would like you to look at it differently for a moment, good guitars are expensive when you compare them to not-so-good guitars. But when you compare them to other standards, they are an incredible bargain. Let's say you like a guitar that costs $2,000. That's a lot of dough in 1986 (our publication year). But wait. . .ompare that to the price of an automobile or a smoker's cigarette bill. You pay five times that amount for a car and it will last you five or six years, maybe. In that time the car will become junk and your guitar which cost five times less will just be coming into its prime. Quit smoking for two years, put the money into a guitar and you've bought somebody's top-of-the-line masterpiece. Or consider what a symphony player spends for a new instrument; fifty or sixty thousand for a fiddle or viola would be a modest price. We are living in some kind of golden age for steel-string guitars. . .the best instruments ever made are being made today, and prices are probably the lowest we shall ever see them to be. Food for thought.

Care of Your Guitar
There are several do's and don'ts you should keep in mind:

- Don't let your guitar get too hot or cold. Cases left in the sun on the seat of a car often warp, crack, or melt glued joints. Car trunks can super-heat an instrument in hot weather too. Very cold temperatures can create finish "checking" (hairline cracks in the laquered finish). The rule is, **avoid very hot or cold temperatures or rapid changes in temperature.**

- Protect your instrument against falling, bumps, collisions with hard objects, and being crushed. Oh, the stories I could tell. To make several long, agonizing stories short: Don't lean the guitar against a wall, it will fall; don't set the case down in the drivway, you'll forget and back over it ; don't leave it in a chair, you'll sit on it; don't wear your belt buckle directly in front, it will scratch away about $400 worth of finish; don't let your guitar come in contact with naugahyde or other plastic upholstery, the solvents are the same in both and a permanently ruinous mar will occur. A friend of mine brought home a brand new Martin D-45, opened the lid of the case, and was horrified to see his baby son throw a set of keys across the room to land squarely on the new guitar. The moral is, **anything can happen.** The rule is, **keep the guitar in the case when not being played.** When it's in the case, **always** close the latches to guard against picking up the case and dumping the instrument out on the ground. These awful things actually happen. A little paranoia is not a bad thing when protecting your guitar.

- Avoid excessive dryness or wetness. Guitars which get too dry in the winter because of artificial heat or in dry climates often develop cracks. Dampness creates warps, finish problems, and separations of glued joints. Humidify in the winter and take an old clunker to the beach or camping in the rain forest. Your good-quality guitar requires moderation in temperature and moisture.

- Watch for any changes or anomolies in the structure of your instrument. One common occurance is that the back edge of the bridge starts to separate from the top. If caught early, this is easily repaired by a competent repair person. Left alone, the top could warp from this seemingly small problem. When you see something suspicious, loosen the strings and make an appointment with your friendly local guitar physician for a check-up. When shipping your instrument or checking it with a commercial airline, loosen strings about 1½-2 steps (about three frets equivalent pitch), use a good hard-shell case, and make sure the guitar fits the case without rattling around inside, yet without stress from anything inside.

- Last, let me encourage you to get close to your guitar and sensitive to it in another way. I still remember the night I had my first guitar. I was twelve and I had never held a guitar in my hands before. It was a mixture of excitement, respect, possibilities, pleasure, and even awe that I felt. I'll never forget it...in fact, I try always to remember it as a good attitude to maintain about the instrument. A guitar is a miracle of wood and steel and glue which embodies stresses and balances so fine it seems as though it should fly apart. But in those finely balanced stresses there is strength, and behind that strength is the possibility of some of the best music in the world. The old-timers back home in Kansas used to say, "I sure love the sound of the old flat-top". Take a close look at your guitar. Think about the music that lies latent behind those steel strings. Let yourself respect its long history. Appreciate the primitive, hands-on quality of the thing. Consider what can come pouring out of the sound hole that is good for the soul, satisfying to the spirit, interesting to the mind, fun for the little kid in us all. Whether your name is Rockefeller or Jones, your guitar is the finest thing you'll ever own.

GUITAR INSTRUCTION & TECHNIQUE

THE GUITAR CHORD SHAPES OF CHARLIE CHRISTIAN
Book/CD Pack
by Joe Weidlich

The concepts and fingerings in this book have been developed by analyzing the licks used by Charlie Christian. Chord shapes are moveable; thus one can play the riffs by simply moving the shape, and fingerings used to play them, up or down the fingerboard. The author shows how the chord shapes – F, D and A – are formed, then can easily be modified to major, minor, dominant seventh and diminished seventh chord voicings.†Analyzing licks frequently used by Charlie Christian, Joe has identified a series of what he calls tetrafragments, i.e., the core element of a lick. The identifiable "sound" of a particular lick is preserved regardless of how many notes are added on either side of it, e.g., pickup notes or tag endings.† Many examples are shown and played on the CD of how this basic concept was used by Charlie Christian to keep his solo lines moving forward. Weidlich also makes observations on the physical manner Charlie Christian used in playing jazz guitar and how that approach contributed to his smooth, mostly down stroke, pick technique.
00000388 Guitar $19.95

GUITAR CHORDS PLUS
by Ron Middlebrook
A comprehensive study of normal and extended chords, tuning, keys, transposing, capo use, and more. Includes over 500 helpful photos and diagrams, a key to guitar symbols, and a glossary of guitar terms.
00000011 ....$11.95

GUITAR TRANSCRIBING – A COMPLETE GUIDE
by Dave Celentano
Learn that solo now! Don't wait for the music to come out – use this complete guide to writing down what you hear. Includes tips, advice, examples and exercises from easy to difficult. Your ear is the top priority and you'll train it to listen more effectively to recognize intervals, chords, note values, counting rhythms and much more for an accurate transcription.
00000378 Book/CD Pack $19.95

GUITAR TUNING FOR THE COMPLETE MUSICAL IDIOT (FOR SMART PEOPLE TOO)
by Ron Middlebrook
A complete book on how to tune up. Contents include: Everything You Need To Know About Tuning; Intonation; Strings; 12-String Tuning; Picks; and much more.
00000002 ....$5.95

INTRODUCTION TO ROOTS GUITAR
by Doug Cox
This book/CD pack by Canada's premier guitar and Dobro° player introduces beginning to°intermediate players to many of the basics of folk/roots guitar. Topics covered include: basic theory, tuning, reading tablature, right- and left-hand patterns, blues rhythms, Travis picking, frailing patterns, flatpicking, open tunings, slide and many more. CD includes 40 demonstration tracks.
00000262 Book/CD Pack $17.95
00000265 VHS Video $19.95

KILLER PENTATONICS FOR GUITAR
by Dave Celentano
Covers innovative and diverse ways of playing pentatonic scales in blues, rock and heavy metal. The licks and ideas in this book will give you a fresh approach to playing the pentatonic scale, hopefully inspiring you to reach for higher levels in your playing. The 37-minute companion CD features recorded examples.
00000285 Book/CD Pack $17.95

LEFT HAND GUITAR CHORD CHART
by Ron Middlebrook
Printed on durable card stock, this "first-of-a-kind" guitar chord chart displays all forms of major and minor chords in two forms, beginner and advanced.
00000005 ....$2.95

MELODIC LINES FOR THE INTERMEDIATE GUITARIST
by Greg Cooper
This book/CD pack is essential for anyone interested in expanding melodic concepts on the guitar. Author Greg Cooper covers: picking exercises; major, minor, dominant and altered lines; blues and jazz turn-arounds; and more.
00000312 Book/CD Pack $19.95

MELODY CHORDS FOR GUITAR
by Allan Holdsworth
Influential fusion player Allan Holdsworth provides guitarists with a simplified method of learning chords, in diagram form, for playing accompaniments and for playing popular melodies in "chord-solo" style. Covers: major, minor, altered, dominant and diminished scale notes in chord form, with lots of helpful reference tables and diagrams.
00000222 ....$19.95

MODAL JAMS AND THEORY
by Dave Celentano
This book shows you how to play the modes, the theory behind mode construction, how to play any mode in any key, how to play the proper mode over a given chord progression, and how to write chord progressions for each of the seven modes. The CD includes two rhythm tracks and a short solo for each mode so guitarists can practice with a "real" band.
00000163 Book/CD Pack $17.95

MONSTER SCALES AND MODES
by Dave Celentano
This book is a complete compilation of scales, modes, exotic scales, and theory. It covers the most common and exotic scales, theory on how they're constructed, and practical applications. No prior music theory knowledge is necessary, since every section is broken down and explained very clearly.
00000140 ....$7.95

OLD TIME COUNTRY GUITAR BACKUP BASICS
by Joseph Weidlich
This instructional book uses commercial recordings from 70 different "sides" from the 1920s and early 1930s as its basis to learn the principal guitar backup techniques commonly used in old-time country music. Topics covered include: boom-chick patterns • bass runs • uses of the pentatonic scale • rhythmic variations • minor chromatic nuances • the use of chromatic passing tones • licks based on chords or chord progressions • and more.
00000389 ....$15.95

OPEN GUITAR TUNINGS
by Ron Middlebrook
This booklet illustrates over 75 different tunings in easy-to-read diagrams. Includes tunings used by artists such as Chet Atkins, Michael Hedges, Jimmy Page, Joe Satriani and more for rock, blues, bluegrass, folk and country styles including open D (for slide guitar), Em, open C, modal tunings and many more.
00000130 ....$4.95

OPEN TUNINGS FOR GUITAR
by Dorian Michael
This book provides 14 folk songs in 9 tunings to help guitarists become comfortable with changing tunings. Songs are ordered so that changing from one tuning to another is logical and non-intrusive. Includes: Fisher Blues (DADGBE) • Fine Toast to Hewlett (DGDGBE) • George Barbazan (DGDGBD) • Amelia (DGDGCD) • Will the Circle Be Unbroken (DADF#AD) • more.
00000224 Book/CD Pack $19.95

ARRANGING FOR OPEN GUITAR TUNINGS
By Dorian Michael
This book/CD pack teaches intermediate-level guitarists how to choose an appropriate tuning for a song, develop an arrangement, and solve any problems that may arise while turning a melody into a guitar piece to play and enjoy.
00000313 Book/CD Pack $19.95

ROCK RHYTHM GUITAR
by Dave Celentano
This helpful book/CD pack cuts out all the confusing technical talk and just gives guitarists the essential tools to get them playing. With Celentano's tips, anyone can build a solid foundation of basic skills to play almost any rhythm guitar style. The exercises and examples are on the CD, in order of difficulty, so players can master new techniques, then move on to more challenging material.
00000274 Book/CD Pack $17.95

SCALES AND MODES IN THE BEGINNING
by Ron Middlebrook
The most comprehensive and complete scale book written especially for the guitar. Chapers include: Fretboard Visualization • Scale Terminology • Scales and Modes • and a Scale to Chord Guide.
00000010 ....$11.95

SLIDE GUITAR AND OPEN TUNINGS
by Doug Cox
Explores the basics of open tunings and slide guitar for the intermediate player, including licks, chords, songs and patterns. This is not just a repertoire book, but rather an approach for guitarists to jam with others, invent their own songs, and understand how to find their way around open tunings with and without a slide. The accompanying CD features 37 tracks.
00000243 Book/CD Pack $17.95

SPEED METAL
by Dave Celentano
In an attempt to teach the aspiring rock guitarist how to pick faster and play more melodically, Dave Celentano uses heavy metal neo-classical styles from Paganini and Bach to rock in this great book/CD pack. The book is structured to take the player through the examples in order of difficulty.
00000261 Book/CD Pack $17.95

25 WAYS TO IMPROVE YOUR SOLO GUITAR PLAYING
by Jay Marks
Keep your music fresh with the great ideas in this new book! Covers: chords, dynamics, harmonics, phrasing, intros & endings and more!
00000323 Book/CD Pack $19.95

Centerstream Publishing, LLC
P.O Box 17878 - Anaheim Hills, CA 92817
P/Fax (714)-779-9390 - Email: Centerstream@aol.com
Website: www.centerstream-usa.com

ACOUSTIC BLUES GUITAR

by Kenny Sultan

This book/CD pack for intermediate-level players incorporates slide or bottleneck playing in both open and standard tunings. All songs are primarily fingerstyle with a monotone bass used for most.
00000157 Book/CD Pack $18.95
00000336 DVD $19.95

BLUES GUITAR
by Kenny Sultan

Through instructional text and actual songs, the author covers blues in five different keys and positions. Covers fingerstyle blues, specific techniques, open tuning, and bottleneck guitar. The CD includes all songs and examples, most played at slow speed and at regular tempo.
00000283 Book/CD Pack $17.95

BLUES GUITAR LEGENDS
by Kenny Sultan

This book/CD pack allows you to explore the styles of Lightnin' Hopkins, Blind Blake, Mississippi John Hurt, Blind Boy Fuller, and Big Bill Broonzy. Through Sultan's arrangements, you will learn how studying the masters can help you develop your own style.
00000181 Book/CD Pack $19.95
00000193 VHS Video $19.95

CHRISTMAS SOUTH OF THE BORDER

featuring the Red Hot Jalapeños with special guest The Cactus Brothers

Add heat to your holiday with these ten salsa-flavored arrangements of time-honored Christmas carols. With the accompanying CD, you can play your guitar along with The Cactus Brothers on: Jingle Bells • Deck the Halls • Silent Night • Joy to the World • What Child Is This? • and more. ¡Feliz Navidad!
00000319 Book/CD Pack $19.95

A CLASSICAL CHRISTMAS

by Ron Middlebrook

This book/CD pack features easy to advanced play-along arrangements of 23 top holiday tunes for classical/fingerstyle guitar. Includes: Birthday of a King • God Rest Ye, Merry Gentlemen • Good Christian Men, Rejoice • Jingle Bells • Joy to the World • O Holy Night • O Sanctissima • What Child Is This? (Greensleeves) • and more. The CD features a demo track for each song.
00000271 Book/CD Pack $15.95

ESSENTIAL BLUES GUITAR

by Dave Celentano

This handy guide to playing blues guitars emphasizes the essentials, such as: chord changes, scales, rhythms, turn arounds, phrasing, soloing and more. Includes lots of examples, plus 10 rhythm tracks for soloing and improvising.
00000237 Book/CD Pack $19.95

FINGERSTYLE GUITAR
by Ken Perlman

Teaches beginning or advanced guitarists how to master the basic musical skills of fingerpicking techniques needed to play folk, blues, fiddle tunes or ragtime on guitar.
00000081 Book Only $24.95
00000175 VHS Video $24.95

THE FLATPICKER'S GUIDE

by Dan Crary

This instruction/method book for flatpicking teaches how to play accompaniments, cross-picking, and how to play lick strums. Examples in the book are explained on the accompanying CD. The CD also allows the player to play along with the songs in the book.
00000231 Book/CD Pack.................$19.95

JAZZ GUITAR CHRISTMAS

by George Ports

Features fun and challenging arrangements of 13 Christmas favorites. Each song is arranged in both easy and intermediate chord melody style. Songs include: All Through the Night • Angels from the Realm of Glory • Away in a Manger • The Boar's Head Carol • The Coventry Carol • Deck the Hall • Jolly Old St. Nicholas • and more.
00000240 ....$9.95

JAZZ GUITAR SOLOS

by George Ports and Frank Sibley

Jazz horn players are some of the best improvisers ever. Now guitarists can learn their tricks! This book features 12 solos (progressing in difficulty) from jazz saxophonists and trumpeters transcribed in easy-to-read guitar tab. The CD features each solo played twice, at slow and regular tempo.
00000188 Book/CD Pack.................$19.95

THE NASTY BLUES
by Tom Ball

A celebration of crude and lewd songs by the best bluesmen and women in history, including Bo Carter, Bessie Smith, Irene Scruggs, Lil Johnson, Georgia White, Charlie Pickett, Lonnie Johnson, Ethel Waters, Dirty Red, and more. 30 songs in all, including: Sam, The Hot Dog Man • I Need a Little Sugar in My Bowl • Send Me a Man • Empty Bed Blues • One Hour Mama • and more.
00000049 ....$12.95

THE PATRIOTIC GUITARIST

arranged by Larry McCabe

This red, white and cool collection contains 22 all-American guitar solos for fingerpickers and flatpickers. Includes: America the Beautiful • The Battle Hymn of the Republic • The Marines' Hymn • The Star Spangled Banner • Yankee Doodle • and many more patriotic favorites. The accompanying CD includes demo tracks for all the tunes.
00000293 Book/CD Pack $19.95

PEDAL STEEL LICKS FOR GUITAR

by Forest Rodgers

Learn to play 30 popular pedal steel licks on the guitar. All examples are played three times on the accompanying CD. Also features tips for the best steel guitar sound reproduction, and steel guitar voiced chords.
00000183 Book/CD Pack......................$16.95
00000348 DVD $19.95

ROCK AROUND THE CLASSICS

by Dave Celentano

This book/CD introduces guitarists of all levels to fresh and innovative ways of playing some of the most popular classical songs. The songs are in order from easiest to most challenging, and a lesson is included on each. Includes: Leyenda • Jesu, Joy of Man's Desiring • Prelude in C# Major • Toccata and Fugue in D Minor • Canon in D Major • more.
00000205 Book/CD Pack...................$19.95

THE SOUND AND FEEL OF BLUES GUITAR
by John Tapella

This comprehensive blues book features information on rhythm patterns, fingerpicking patterns, double stops, licks in A, D, E, and G, and more. The accompanying CD features several compositions and all examples in the book.
00000092 Book/CD Pack $17.95

SURF GUITAR
by Dave Celentano

This totally tubular book/CD pack gives you all the tools to play convincing surf guitar, covering concepts, techniques, equipment and even surf slang! At the core of the book are six original surf songs by The Torquays. You can play along with these six tunes on the accompanying CD, and for each one, the book includes a transcription, lesson and analysis.
00000279 Book/CD Pack $22.95

THIS IS THE TIME – THE DILLARDS SONGBOOK COLLECTION

This songbook features classic songs from 40 great years of bluegrass by the Dillards. Contains many of their most requested songs, including those performed by The Darlins' on the *Andy Griffith Show*.
00000382 ....$19.95

VIRGINIA REELS

by Joseph Weidlich

This unique book/CD pack features basic fingerstyle guitar arrangements of 35 songs originally arranged for pianoforte in George Willig, Jr.'s book *Virginia Reels*, published in Baltimore in 1839. The accompanying CD features all of the songs recorded at medium tempo and played in their entirety, and the book includes helpful performance notes.
00000241 Book/CD Pack $17.95

Book's and DVD's from Centerstream Publishing

P.O Box 17878- Anaheim Hills, CA 92817

centerstrm@aol.com